DARK PSYCHOLOGY DECODED: TL;DR - THE QUICK & DIRTY

DEFEND YOURSELF AGAINST MANIPULATION

TL;DR™ - THE QUICK & DIRTY SERIES
BOOK 1

WYNNE WICK

For everyone who thinks "reading" means skimming bullet points ...

and "learning" means watching one more YouTube explainer ...

You're my people.

This cheat code's for you. This is your shortcut to street smarts.

No fluff. No filters. All fire. 🔥

CONTENTS

INTRODUCTION

> *"There are only two types of people who discourage others from learning manipulation: naive people and manipulators. We highly recommend you ignore both."*
>
> ~ Lucio Buffalmano

Hey, what's the summary of this Intro? 🤔

Well, here's the Quick & Dirty: Welcome to the Shadow Side of Human Influence 👥 You'll be shocked when you find out what's really going on behind the scenes …

YOU'VE BEEN PLAYED—NOW IT'S TIME TO SEE THE GAMEBOARD

You know the type: that coworker who always walks away with the win, the partner who chips away at your confidence, or the friend who suddenly ropes you into something that wasn't part of the plan. What do they all have in common?

They're using dark psychology; sometimes consciously, sometimes instinctively. It's not magic. It's **manipulation in plain sight.** 👀

Let's open with real-life examples—scenarios that seem harmless on the surface but reveal something far more insidious beneath:

- A charming office manipulator effortlessly pulls strings behind the scenes.
- A partner gaslights their significant other, leaving them questioning their reality.
- A friend frames a "catch-up lunch" as an opportunity to push their agenda.

These are the realms of dark psychology where persuasion becomes coercion, and influence turns into control.

🔮 WHAT IS DARK PSYCHOLOGY?

- Dark psychology refers to the use of psychological principles —typically meant for connection, communication, or leadership—for **deception, manipulation, and control.**
- It is **covert, calculated, and powerful**, operating silently in everyday environments.
- **It is found everywhere:** boardrooms, bedrooms, breakrooms, and beyond.

👉 *Without awareness, you become an **unwitting participant** in someone else's game.*

WHY THIS BOOK EXISTS

Unlike surface-level self-help or entry-level persuasion guides, "Dark Psychology Decoded: TL;DR - The Quick & Dirty" is:

- A **deep-dive manual** into the inner workings of psychological manipulation.
- Your **toolkit** for decoding and defending against subtle control.
- A **guide to ethical influence**, self-empowerment, and boundary-setting.
- And it's all wrapped up in quick, easy to digest, bullet points of the best info you need.

👉 *This is a book for those who want to **understand the game, not be played by it**, and they want it NOW.*

HOW THIS BOOK IS STRUCTURED

You're not just learning theory. You're building layered skills chapter by chapter:

1. 🖋 **Foundation & Psychological Profiles:** Learn key psychological models (like the Big Five, HEXACO, Dark Triad) and what motivates

manipulative personalities.

2. 🤘 **Body Language Mastery:** Decode nonverbal cues, micro-expressions, facial tells, and the hidden choreography of influence.

3. 🕵️ **Lie Detection:** Unmask deception using verbal and nonverbal red flags, interrogation models, and your personal lie detection radar.

4. 🥺 **Emotional Manipulation:** Spot gaslighting, guilt-tripping, emotional blackmail, and coercion—then defend your mental space.

5. 🤫 **Covert Influence Techniques:** Explore advanced tactics like social proof, scarcity, anchoring, and psychological warfare.

6. 🧠 **Mind Control & NLP:** Tap into conversational hypnosis, anchoring, embedded commands, and ethical use of influence.

7. 📱 **Social Media & Digital Manipulation:** Understand how algorithms, influencers, and curated content distort your digital reality.

8. 🌍 **Real-World Scenarios:** Examine how manipulation plays out in politics, marketing, cults, and competitive dynamics.

9. 🛡️ **Defensive and Empowerment Strategies:** Build resilience, set strong boundaries, and master ethical persuasion for personal growth and leadership.

———————

👉 *These chapters are filled with **interactive tools**—reflections, journaling prompts, takeaways, and real world case examples.*

———————

IS THIS BOOK FOR YOU?

🙌 This book is your perfect fit if you've ever:

- Felt drained or confused after conversations with certain people.
- Wondered why some people always seem to get their way (even when they're wrong).
- Lost your voice in relationships or workplaces.
- Suspected manipulation but couldn't quite name it or prove it.
- Wanted to develop deeper **emotional resilience** and **self-awareness**.

💡 **Spoiler Alert:** If you've had any of those thoughts, you're already intuitive. This book will sharpen that intuition into insight and action.

WHAT YOU'LL GAIN

By the end of this journey, you will:

- **Recognize manipulation instantly**, even when it's cloaked in charm or flattery.
- Build **mental and emotional defenses** that are unshakeable.
- Understand **why people manipulate** what makes you vulnerable, and how to stop it.
- Develop **authentic influence skills** without ever crossing ethical lines.
- Feel **confident, calm, and clear** in your decisions and communication.

COMMON SKEPTICISM

You might be wondering: "Can I really learn to detect and deflect manipulation like a pro?"

🧠 YES. Hundreds of others who once doubted themselves now:

- See manipulation coming from miles away.
- Handle toxic situations with clarity.
- Protect their boundaries without guilt or second-guessing.

📝 **Note:** You're not being asked to believe blindly. You're being given **evidence-based tools**, crafted through psychological research and real-world examples.

👉 *Takeaway: Skepticism is healthy. Use it to question, analyze, and grow.*

INTERACTIVE TOOLS TO SUPERCHARGE YOUR LEARNING

This book includes:

- 🧠 Reflective Journaling Prompts
- 🎯 Real-World Applications
- 📱 Bonus Content

✅ These features are designed to help you absorb and apply your skills **immediately**—not just after you've finished reading.

🌱 **A New Version of You**

This isn't about turning into a manipulator. It's about becoming:

- **Unshakable** in the face of mind games
- **Empowered** to communicate clearly
- **Equipped** to build authentic influence
- **In control** of your decisions and emotional responses

👉 *Once you decode dark psychology, you're no longer the one being played. You're the one **writing your own script**.*

🔑 FINAL TAKEAWAYS FROM THE INTRODUCTION

- ✅ **Dark psychology is everywhere**, often invisible to the untrained eye.
- ✅ **This book is your decoder ring**—revealing what's really happening behind the words, smiles, and subtle cues.
- ✅ **Manipulation thrives in ignorance.** But now, you're stepping into awareness.
- ✅ **You can't change the world (or your own life) until you understand how it works.** This is your blueprint.

🎯 **Call to Action:**

Step into the next chapter. Decode the tactics. Arm yourself. And emerge stronger, smarter, and sharper. 💪

CHAPTER 1
DECODING DARK PSYCHOLOGY

" *"You are a manipulator. I like to think of myself more as an outcome engineer."*

~ J.R. Ward

Hey, ISO the chapter summary for "Decoding Dark Psychology"? Can you help me out? 😎

You know it! So, this chapter starts with the typical situation (I can relate! NGL): a subtle, guilt-laced comment at a family brunch. 🙄 This scene is used to introduce you to the essence of dark psychology—an often invisible, covert form of psychological influence used to control others through manipulation, guilt, fear, emotional appeals, and persuasion. These tactics don't always stem from malicious intent; sometimes they're used unconsciously. But regardless of motivation, they can have significant effects on your decisions, emotions, and behavior.

🤔 UNDERSTANDING DARK PSYCHOLOGY

Dark psychology refers to the study and use of psychological principles to manipulate, deceive, and exploit others. While traditional psychology is concerned with understanding and improving human behavior, dark psychology focuses on influence, control, and power, often used unethically.

It's commonly misunderstood as the domain of villains or sociopaths, but the truth is more disturbing—it's present in everyday life. Anyone can use these tactics, knowingly or not: parents, friends, coworkers, influencers, and romantic partners.

Common Examples in Daily Life

Dark psychology hides in plain sight:

- **Relationships:** One partner may use guilt or avoidance to control discussions or deflect blame.
- **Workplaces:** Gaslighting and undermining confidence are common forms of manipulation.
- **Media and advertising:** Psychological triggers subtly influence consumer behavior without the audience realizing it.

👉 *This chapter's mission is to empower you to identify and protect yourself from such insidious tactics.*

✏ KEY PSYCHOLOGICAL THEORIES BEHIND MANIPULATION

The chapter covers the core psychological concepts that form the foundation of manipulative techniques.

1. Classical Conditioning (Pavlov) 🔔

This principle is about associating one stimulus with another. If someone consistently links a sound, smell, or gesture with a feeling (comfort, fear, love), they can use this association to steer your behavior or emotional state.

Example: A manipulator could use a certain tone or phrase that you've come to associate with approval or disapproval to provoke compliance.

2. Social Learning Theory (Bandura) 📚

We often learn behaviors by watching others. Media, authority figures, or peer groups shape our ideas of what's acceptable. Manipulators often model charismatic behavior, mirroring respected figures, to gain trust or influence.

Example: A colleague mimics the authoritative body language of a boss to influence a meeting.

3. Cognitive Dissonance (Festinger) 💬

When our beliefs and actions don't align, we feel discomfort, called cognitive dissonance. Manipulators exploit this by putting people in situations where they feel compelled to change their attitudes or actions to ease the internal tension.

Example: A jury member gives in to a group decision they disagree with to avoid being the outlier.

. . .

4. Cognitive Biases (Tversky & Kahneman) 🤯

Our brains rely on shortcuts—called biases—that can distort decision-making. Manipulators exploit biases like:

- **Confirmation Bias:** We favor information that supports our beliefs.
- **Halo Effect:** A positive trait in one area (e.g., attractiveness) makes us overlook flaws in another.
- **Emotional Arousal:** Heightened emotion weakens logic and increases suggestibility.

👉 *These mental patterns can be manipulated to influence decisions without direct pressure.*

💡 THE POWER OF EMOTIONAL INTELLIGENCE

Emotional intelligence (EI) is a vital skill that helps you decode emotions—yours and others'. It includes four pillars:

1. **Self-Awareness:** Understanding your own emotions, triggers, and behavioral patterns.

2. **Self-Regulation:** The ability to control your responses and remain calm under pressure.

3. **Empathy:** The skill of reading others' emotions accurately.

4. **Social Skills:** Managing relationships, communication, and conflict constructively.

. . .

EI can be used for good, like when building trust and understanding. But in the hands of manipulators, it becomes a weapon. Emotionally intelligent people can detect insecurities and subtly guide your behavior using flattery, concern, or subtle pressure. 👹

Example: A manager who notices your anxiety might exaggerate expectations to keep you overworking, making you feel like you're never enough.

🧘 STRENGTHENING EMOTIONAL INTELLIGENCE FOR SELF DEFENSE

To defend against dark psychology tactics, strengthen your own EI. Here's how it's done:

- 🧘 **Mindfulness:** Helps you remain aware of emotions and react calmly.
- 🤸 **Empathy with Boundaries:** Understand others without sacrificing yourself.
- 🌐 **Self-Reflection:** Journaling and introspection help uncover emotional triggers and manipulation patterns.
- 💡 **Active Listening:** Listen carefully and look for inconsistencies between words and tone, which often reveal manipulation.

⚖ THE ETHICAL USE OF PSYCHOLOGICAL POWER

> *"With great power comes great responsibility." ~Attributed to Peter Parker's Uncle Ben from "Spider-Man"*

Just because you understand these tools doesn't mean they should be used unethically. Manipulative power can be seductive, but it's critical to develop a personal code of ethics. Reflective questions can help guide ethical behavior:

- What do I gain?
- What might others lose?
- Is this tactic helpful or harmful in the long run?

☛ *Ethical influence inspires, uplifts, and respects autonomy. It builds sustainable trust—in business, relationships, and teaching. The goal is empowerment, not control.*

🗡 FINAL THOUGHTS

The takeaway? Dark psychology is everywhere. But once you learn the patterns, you'll see the puppet strings—and you'll cut them before they wrap around you.

This chapter provides your first "X-ray vision" into psychological warfare, making the unseen visible. Through stories, studies, and action steps, it transforms fear into awareness, and awareness into empowerment. 💪

◎˙BULLSEYE RECAP

✅ What is Dark Psychology?

It's the use of psychological tactics to influence, deceive, or control others.

- Occurs in relationships, workplaces, media, and daily interactions.
- Is often subtle, sometimes unconscious.

✅ Core Manipulation Theories

- **Classical Conditioning:** Associating stimuli with emotional states.
- **Social Learning Theory:** Mimicking respected figures or peers.
- **Cognitive Dissonance:** Changing beliefs or actions to reduce discomfort.
- **Cognitive Biases:** Exploiting mental shortcuts like confirmation bias and emotional decision-making.

✅ Emotional Intelligence (EI)

- Is a key defense against manipulation.
- Includes self-awareness, regulation, empathy, and social skills.
- Can be used ethically—or as a tool of manipulation.

✅ Defensive Techniques

- **Mindfulness:** Stay present and calm under pressure.
- **Journaling & Reflection:** Uncover emotional patterns and triggers

- **Empathetic Distance:** Understand others without absorbing their emotions.
- **Active Listening:** Catch subtle manipulation or emotional inconsistencies.

✅ Ethics of Influence

- Influence without integrity is coercion.
- Ask: "Does this serve both me and others?"
- Leaders, teachers, and professionals must use influence responsibly.

💥 *The Quick & Dirty*
** *Dark psychology is real—and common.*
** *You're likely being influenced in ways you don't see (yet).*
** *Awareness, emotional intelligence, and ethical clarity are your strongest defense tools.*

CHAPTER 2
ANALYZING HUMAN BEHAVIORAL PSYCHOLOGY

66 *"Human behavior flows from three main sources: desire, emotion, and knowledge."*

~ Plato

Hey, what's the chapter About for "Analyzing Human Behavioral Psychology"? 👀

So, FYI turns out that human behavior is driven by desire, emotion, and knowledge— Plato's timeless insight still rings true in today's psychological landscape. This chapter reveals what motivates people, especially those who use covert or manipulative tactics to get their way. It unpacks the darker side of personality, revealing how traits like narcissism, Machiavellianism, and psychopathy (collectively known as the Dark Triad ▲) influence behavior and relationships.

These traits often hide behind charm, competence, or charisma. But if you know what to look for, you can recognize them, guard against their tactics, and even use psychological tools like personality profiling to gain insight into others.

▲ THE DARK TRIAD

The "Dark Triad" refers to three personality traits known for their manipulative potential:

1. Narcissism

- Is obsessed with admiration, status, and self-image.
- Is entitled, grandiose, and image-conscious.
- Is often charming, but lacks genuine empathy.

2. Machiavellianism

- Is strategic, cunning, and manipulative.
- Is goal-oriented without regard for ethics.
- Uses flattery, deceit, and calculated moves.

3. Psychopathy

- Lacks empathy and remorse.
- Is cold, calm under pressure, and emotionally detached.
- Often gaslights, lies effortlessly, and uses others without guilt.

📝 Additionally, **sociopathy** is introduced as a "wild card," combining elements from all three. Sociopaths are impulsive, aggressive, and often disregard social norms entirely.

► RECOGNIZING RED FLAGS

These individuals often hide behind polished personas. But their patterns leak through:

- **Narcissists:** Interrupt frequently, resist criticism, dominate conversations, and crave admiration.
- **Machiavellians:** Manipulate behind the scenes, form alliances for personal gain, and lack genuine emotional connection.
- **Psychopaths:** Mimic emotions but don't feel them, stay eerily calm in chaos, and exploit others without remorse.

☀ WHAT DRIVES MANIPULATION?

Understanding manipulative behavior requires examining core human needs and psychological frameworks.

Maslow's Hierarchy of Needs:

Manipulators often act out when their basic or emotional needs go unmet:

- **Safety Needs:** Job security, financial stability
- **Belonging Needs:** Acceptance, love, approval
- **Esteem Needs:** Status, recognition, validation
- **Self-Actualization:** Control, autonomy, purpose

☞ *If these needs feel threatened, manipulation becomes a shortcut to satisfying them.*

Power & Insecurity

- Power offers control over resources, people, or emotions.
- Insecurity often fuels bullying, lying, or emotional sabotage.
- Fear of abandonment can lead to controlling or emotionally dependent behavior.

👉 *Manipulation often boils down to avoiding pain or chasing pleasure— whether it's security, approval, or influence.*

🎭 PERSONALITY PROFILING: SEEING BEHIND THE MASK

Profiling personalities helps you anticipate reactions and decode hidden motives. In high-stakes social dynamics, this is invaluable.

Informal vs. Formal Profiling:

- Observe behavior, communication style, and stress responses.
- For formal profiling, use assessments like:
    - Myers-Briggs
    - Enneagram
    - DISC
    - MMPI
    - 16PF
    - HEXACO (focuses on dark traits)

The Big Five Traits:

1. **Openness**—Imaginative vs. Conventional

2. **Conscientiousness**—Disciplined vs. Careless

3. **Extraversion**—Outgoing vs. Reserved

4. **Agreeableness**—Compassionate vs. Critical

5. **Neuroticism**—Emotionally Reactive vs. Stable

The HEXACO Model (adds Honesty-Humility):

- Adds the "**H Factor**" (honesty and humility) to reveal levels of sincerity, loyalty, fairness, and modesty.
- Low H = higher tendency for manipulation and unethical behavior.
- HEXACO is a better predictor of Dark Triad traits.

📝 Use profiling ethically to build trust, not manipulate. Context also matters—how someone acts under stress may differ from how they present themselves casually.

🧩 **Honesty-Humility (H Factor): A Key to Dark Traits**

This trait is the opposite of the Dark Triad.

- **High H:** Sincere, honest, fair, rule-following
- **Low H:** Deceitful, greedy, arrogant, and manipulative

Traits from the H factor align closely with altruism, integrity, and empathy—while low scores correlate with exploitative or sociopathic behavior.

When assessing yourself or others, this scale can highlight vulnerabilities (who is easily manipulated) and point out potential threats (who is likely to manipulate).

🎯 BULLSEYE RECAP

✅ The Dark Triad Plus 🔱

- **Narcissism** = Ego, image control, entitlement
- **Machiavellianism** = Strategic deception, power over people
- **Psychopathy** = Cold, manipulative, guilt-free
- **Sociopathy** = Impulsive, aggressive, anti-social tendencies

✅ How to Spot Them 👀

- ▶ **Red Flags:**
  - Interrupting
  - Flattery
  - Avoidance of accountability
  - Emotional coldness
  - Gaslighting
  - Excessive charisma masking insecurity

✅ Why People Manipulate ❓

- Have unmet needs (Maslow): survival, love, esteem
- Have a desire for power and control.
- Are insecure or fear rejection.
- Childhood conditioning and learned behaviors.
- Escape pain, chase pleasure.

✅ Defense Against Manipulation 🛡

- Set and enforce **boundaries.**
- Build **emotional intelligence** and **self-awareness.**
- Watch for manipulation of needs or fears.
- Trust your **gut instincts** when something feels "**off.**"

- Lean on a **support system** for feedback and perspective.

✅ Profiling Tools 💼

- **Big Five (OCEAN):** Personality trait spectrum
- **HEXACO:** Adds H Factor (honesty & humility)
- **Use tests** like MBTI, MMPI, 16PF, Enneagram, DISC
- Interpret results in **context**—personality is dynamic.

✅ The Power of the H Factor 🔋

- **High H** = trustworthiness, fairness, modesty
- **Low H** = prone to lying, cheating, exploiting others
- **HEXACO** is the go-to model for assessing dark tendencies.

💥 _The Quick & Dirty_

1. Human behavior is driven by needs and shaped by personality.
2. The Dark Triad traits are charming but dangerous—learn to spot them.
3. Manipulative behavior often stems from fear, insecurity, or unmet emotional needs.
4. Profiling helps you read people more clearly and anticipate behavior.
5. The H factor in HEXACO is essential for detecting manipulation risk.
6. Your best defense is awareness, boundaries, and emotional intelligence.

CHAPTER 3

MASTERING NON-VERBAL INFLUENCE BODY LANGUAGE

> " *"The most important thing in communication is hearing what isn't said."*
>
> ~ Peter F. Drucker

Hey, what's the chapter summary for Mastering Non-Verbal Influence? 🤪

So, AAMOF words may convey ideas, but body language reveals truth. 😎 In this chapter, we dive deep into the powerful world of non-verbal communication—where micro-expressions, posture, eye contact, gestures, and even the direction of your feet speak louder than your voice. Whether you're reading others, or mastering your own presence, understanding body language provides a profound advantage in personal, social, and professional arenas.

Non-verbal cues include facial expressions, gestures, posture, touch, space, and micro-expressions. These signals can reinforce verbal messages—or completely contradict them. Learning to **read body language accurately** and **controlling your own non-verbal signals** gives you the upper hand in interpreting intent, influencing perception, detecting deception, and building rapport.

👁 THE LANGUAGE OF THE UNSPOKEN

🗣 **Non-Verbal Basics:**

- **Facial Expressions** are universal (e.g., fear, anger, happiness).
- **Gestures** reveal emotional states.
- **Posture** communicates confidence or submission.
- **Eye Contact** builds trust—or can betray discomfort.
- **Touch and Proximity** impact how relationships are formed and maintained.

🤟 **Dual Responsibility:**

- Learn to **read** others' signals.
- Learn to **project** authenticity, confidence, and control through your own body language.

👀 EYE CONTACT: INTENTIONS IN A GLANCE

- **Direct Eye Contact** = engagement, honesty, confidence.
- **Averted Gaze** = discomfort, dishonesty, insecurity.

- **Too Much** = intimidation or creepiness.
- **Synchronizing** eye movement subtly builds trust.
- **Cultural Cues Matter**—in some cultures, direct eye contact is rude or aggressive.

👉 *Detecting deceit: Inconsistent eye behavior (avoiding gaze, excessive blinking, unnatural stare) often points to lying. Watch for changes in **baseline behavior**.*

🧍 POSTURE & POWER

Posture Silently Announces:

- Confidence
- Insecurity
- Authority
- Engagement or detachment

Confident Posture Includes:

- Upright spine
- Open stance
- Relaxed shoulders
- Balanced weight distribution

Situational Use:

- Job interviews or negotiations: Use "power poses."
- Public speaking: Stand tall, open arms, eye contact.
- Casual settings: Relaxed but alert posture shows ease and approachability.

Practice with:

- Wall Alignment Check
- Seated Posture Reset
- Power poses like the "Superman" stance

🤝 TOUCH & PROXEMICS (SPATIAL AWARENESS)

Touch conveys support, connection, or dominance.

Examples: handshake (professional), hug (personal), pat on the back (support).

Use appropriately based on context and relationship. **Proxemics** is about the space between people:

- **Intimate** (0–18 inches): Close relationships
- **Personal** (1.5–4 ft): Friends, casual interactions
- **Social** (4–12 ft): Workplace, acquaintances
- **Public** (12+ ft): Public speaking, strangers

👉 *Closing Distance = Interest*

👉 *Backing Off = Discomfort*

👣 FEET: THE SECRET TRUTH-TELLERS

Feet are harder to consciously control, making them reliable indicators:

- **Feet Pointed at You** = Engagement
- **Feet Angled Away** = Disinterest or Desire to Exit
- **Tapping/Bouncing** = Anxiety or Impatience
- **Mirrored Foot Positioning** = Rapport

⭐ Watch for discrepancies between words and feet—often, the feet tell the truth.

🖐 GESTURES & MIRRORING

Gestures support or sabotage your spoken message:

- **Open Gestures** = Receptiveness, Trust
- **Closed Gestures** (Crossed Arms, Clenched Fists) = Defensiveness, Discomfort
- **Fidgeting** = Nerves or Dishonesty
- **Deliberate Hand Movements** = Confidence and Control

👉 *Mirroring (subtly mimicking body language) builds subconscious rapport, signaling similarity and trust. Don't overdo it—it should be natural and subtle.*

🙂 Micro-Expressions: Split-Second Truths

Micro-expressions are involuntary facial flashes that betray:

- 😡 Anger (tight lips, flared nostrils)
- 😯 Surprise (raised eyebrows)
- 🤢 Disgust (wrinkled nose)

- 😱 Fear (open mouth, pulled-back head)
- 😏 Contempt (smirk)
- 🥺 Sadness (downturned lips)

They last fractions of a second, making them hard to fake or suppress. These expressions:

- Reveal suppressed emotions.
- Help detect deception.
- Signal underlying thoughts.

👉 *Train to recognize these cues by watching movies on mute, analyzing real-life interactions, or practicing with feedback from others.*

😊 **Manipulating Facial Cues & Using Expressions Defensively**

- **Align facial expressions** with your words to appear credible.
- **Deliberately manage expressions** in high-stakes situations (e.g., neutral face in tense meetings).
- **Use visualization & breathing techniques** to regulate expressions under pressure.
- Practice **role-playing** to enhance your response control.

👉 *When used ethically, facial control enhances persuasion, confidence, and authority. In dark psychology, it can be weaponized for manipulation—use it wisely.*

💼 APPLICATION: BODY LANGUAGE IN ACTION

In Business:

- Read room reactions.
- Note tension (crossed arms, tight expressions).
- Engage disengaged listeners with openness and movement.
- Shift your strategy based on the signals you observe.

In Social Situations:

- Tune into inconsistencies.
- Spot fake smiles or "happy masks."
- Watch for dominant posture shifts or sudden withdrawal.

🎯 BULLSEYE RECAP

✅ **Master Non-Verbal Communication**

- 93% of communication is non-verbal.
- Body language includes facial expressions, posture, gestures, touch, space, and micro-expressions.

✅ **Eye Contact**

- Builds trust and confidence.
- Must be balanced and culturally appropriate.
- Irregularities often signal deceit.

✅ **Posture**

- Signals power, vulnerability, interest, or disengagement.
- Use "power poses" in high-stakes settings.

✅ Touch & Space

- Touch can bond or intimidate—context matters.
- Respect personal space zones; use proximity intentionally.

✅ Gestures

- Open = safe, confident.
- Closed = defensive, anxious.
- Use gestures to reinforce speech.

✅ Micro-Expressions

- Reveal real emotions beneath the surface.
- Can't be controlled—learn to spot them for emotional truth.

✅ Facial Expressions as Tools

- Align your facial cues with your message.
- Use neutral or confident expressions to project control.
- Practice to gain mastery.

💥 Quick & Dirty

1. Non-verbal communication is your most powerful influence tool—often more impactful than speech.

2. Reading body language helps uncover hidden emotions, intentions, and deception.

3. Mastering your own non-verbal cues boosts credibility, trust, and confidence in any interaction.

4. Posture, eye contact, facial expressions, and gestures must align with your message for maximum impact.

5. Practice and observation sharpen your decoding skills, giving you a strategic advantage in both defense and persuasion.

6. Use this power ethically—awareness is empowerment, not an excuse for exploitation.

CHAPTER 4
DETECTING DECEPTION
AND UNMASKING

> *"I'm not upset that you lied to me; I'm upset that from now on, I can't believe you."*
>
> ~ Friedrich Nietzsche

Hey, what's the chapter summary for "Detecting Deception and Unmasking Lies"? TIA 😱

So, JSYK lying is (sadly) a part of everyday life 😨—but when does it become manipulation? This chapter takes a deep dive into the psychology of deception, exploring why people lie, the different types of liars, how to detect lies through observation, and how to build your own lie detection toolkit.

Lies come in many shades—from white lies meant to avoid discomfort, to strategic fabrications used to gain power or control. The chapter explores **liar typologies**, delves into **motivations behind lying**, examines **verbal and non-verbal deception cues**, and contrasts **interrogation strategies** like the controversial Reid Technique and ethical PEACE Method. It also introduces emerging **AI technologies** and guides you through building your **personal deception detection toolkit**—combining intuition, observation, and strategy.

👉 *The ability to detect deceit is one of the most powerful tools in your psychological arsenal.*

👤 TYPES OF LIARS

Pathological Liars

- Lie compulsively and often unnecessarily.
- Originates in childhood; may involve a dissociation from reality.
- Often fabricate elaborate stories for attention or sympathy.
- Lose track of their own fabrications.

Situational Liars

- Lie in response to specific pressures (e.g., to avoid punishment or gain an advantage).
- View lies as "white" or "harmless."
- Motivated by fear, avoidance, or self-preservation.

💡 WHY PEOPLE LIE: PSYCHOLOGICAL MOTIVATIONS

Ego Protection – To avoid shame or preserve reputation.

Social Acceptance – To fit in, impress others, or gain admiration.

Control & Power – To manipulate people and outcomes.

Fear – Of rejection, punishment, or conflict.

Gain – To win, achieve goals, or gain an advantage.

Avoidance – Of responsibility, confrontation, or negative consequences.

👉 *Many lies are driven by unmet psychological needs or insecurity. Liars must constantly work to maintain the illusion, often leading to eventual exposure.*

✏️ DETECTING LIES: TOOLS AND TECHNIQUES

🔍 Establish a Baseline

- Observe a person's normal communication style when relaxed and truthful.
- Look for deviations: hesitations, changes in tone, mismatched gestures.

💬 Verbal Clues

- Hesitation, filler words ("um," "uh"), or stalling.
- Inconsistent details or changes in story upon retelling.

37

- Overly detailed or overly vague responses.
- Defensive responses like "Why would I lie?"

😠 **Non-Verbal Clues**

- Micro-expressions: involuntary flashes of guilt, fear, or contempt.
- Incongruent gestures: shaking head "no" while saying "yes."
- Eye aversion or overcompensation with intense eye contact.
- Self-soothing: touching face, neck, fidgeting.
- Shifts in posture or increased physical distance.

⁉️ ADVANCED INTERROGATION TECHNIQUES

🔴 **Reid Technique (Traditional, Coercive)**

- Used in law enforcement to elicit confessions.
- Includes 9 steps such as confrontation, stopping denials, creating alternative narratives.
- Focuses on psychological pressure, breaking down defenses.
- Criticized for causing **false confessions**.

🧘 **PEACE Method (Ethical, Non-Confrontational)**

- Originated in the UK; emphasizes rapport and evidence-based questioning.
- 5 Phases: Preparation, Engage, Account, Closure, Evaluate.
- Encourages honesty through transparency and respect.
- Reduces risk of manipulation and false confessions.

👲 **Lie Detection & Technology**

- **Polygraphs** detect physiological stress—not lies directly.

- **AI + Biometric Tools** analyze micro-expressions, voice stress, speech patterns.
- **Pros:** Speed, pattern recognition, scale.
- **Cons:** Bias, false positives, lack of emotional nuance.

👉 *Tech tools should **augment human observation**, not replace it.*

🚩 COMMON RED FLAGS OF DECEPTION

- Inconsistency in stories
- Emotional mismatch (smiling when sad; laughing when serious)
- Over-embellishment or deflection
- Sudden silence or emotional withdrawal
- Physical discomfort signals (sweating, shifting weight, crossing arms)
- Cognitive load indicators (confusion, contradiction, memory gaps)

👉 *The more complex the lie, the more likely the liar will slip up.*

🛠 BUILDING YOUR DECEPTION DETECTION TOOLKIT

1. Intuition

- Trust your gut—your subconscious picks up on inconsistencies.
- Sharpen awareness with mindfulness and presence.

2. Observation Practice

- Watch people in public without listening to conversation.
- Track gestures, facial expressions, shifts in body language.
- Journal patterns you notice.

3. Role Playing

- Practice being both the deceiver and the detector.
- Analyze reactions and observe real-time feedback.

4. Cognitive Techniques

- Increase cognitive load: ask detailed or unexpected questions.
- Test for consistency across repeated storytelling.
- Challenge vague answers or diversions.

🎯 Bullseye Recap

✅ Liars & Lies

- Pathological Liars: compulsive, chronic, irrational
- Situational Liars: reactive, strategic, context-driven
- Motivations include ego protection, approval, fear, power, and gain.

✅ Deception Detection

- Establish behavioral baselines.
- Note verbal shifts: stalling, contradictions, excessive detail.
- Watch for non-verbal leaks: micro-expressions, nervous gestures, eye behavior.
- Trust your instincts—emotions often don't lie, even if words do.

✅ Interrogation Techniques

- **Reid Technique:** pressure-based, manipulative
- **PEACE Method:** respectful, ethical, rapport-driven
- Use open-ended questions to uncover truth.

✅ Red Flags

- Emotional over- or under-reaction.
- Shifts in speech tone, rate, or detail.
- Sudden physical withdrawal or fidgeting.
- Conflicting facial cues or eye movement patterns.
- "Too good to be true" or oddly vague stories.

✅ Toolkit Development

- Practice active observation.
- Train intuition with mindfulness.
- Apply questioning strategies to test for inconsistencies.
- Keep a deception log to spot patterns.

☀ *The Quick & Dirty*

1. Not all lies are created equally—understand the types and motives behind deception.

2. Baseline behavior is your lie detector foundation. Observe, then compare.

3. Micro-expressions and subtle cues often betray the truth.

4. Cognitive load and storytelling inconsistencies are major cracks in the liar's mask.

5. Ethical questioning (like the PEACE method) is more effective and respectful than coercion.

6. AI and biometrics are tools, not replacements—use them in tandem with human intuition.

7. The best deception detector blends sharp observation with strategic questioning.

CHAPTER 5
EMOTIONAL MANIPULATION TECHNIQUES

> *"Manipulation thrives in an environment of uncertainty and fear."*
>
> ~ Brené Brown, *Daring Greatly (2012)*

Hey, I just wanted to AA the chapter summary for "Emotional Manipulation Techniques"! 💔

Well, emotional manipulation is ABT the art of using someone's empathy, fears, and emotional responses against them for control. While it can appear subtle and even caring on the surface, emotional manipulation is one of the most destructive forms of psychological influence. It thrives in environments of fear, uncertainty, and imbalance. 😳

The chapter shows real-life examples of manipulation—such as social media guilt-tripping or emotionally exhausting friendships—before breaking down a full suite of tactics from the **Manipulator's Toolbox**. From gaslighting to guilt-tripping, manipulators expertly prey on your emotional vulnerabilities, often keeping you in cycles of confusion, dependency, and self-doubt. They know your triggers and use them as weapons to extract compliance and control.

🧰 THE MANIPULATOR'S TOOLBOX: 13 CORE TACTICS

1. 🥴 Gaslighting

- Undermines your perception of reality.
- Makes you doubt your memory, sanity, or judgment.
- "You're imagining things" or "You're too sensitive" are common phrases.

2. 🤥 Paltering

- Telling half-truths or using truthful statements to mislead.
- "Technically true" but omits critical context.
- Common in business, politics, and passive-aggressive social interactions.

3. 🔪 Backstabbing

- Two-faced behavior that undermines you while feigning support.
- Creates distrust and confusion within groups or relationships.

4. 🌑 Love Bombing

- Intense adoration early in a relationship, followed by devaluation.
- Creates emotional dependency and guilt when affection is later withdrawn.

5. 😰 Silent Treatment

- Refusing to communicate to punish or control.
- Triggers anxiety and forces the victim to seek reconnection, often at the cost of self-respect.

6. 🗣 Negging

- Backhanded compliments or subtle put-downs to lower your self-esteem.
- Keeps you seeking the manipulator's approval.

7. ✂ Isolation

- Gradually cutting you off from support systems.
- Increases dependency and reduces your ability to seek help or perspective.

8. ⚠ Triangulation

- Bringing a third party into conflict to create jealousy, rivalry, or confusion.
- Disrupts trust and clarity in relationships.

9. 🎴 Guilt Tripping

- Weaponizing empathy by making you feel responsible for someone else's emotions or problems.

- "After everything I've done for you ..." is a classic line.

10. 🥺 Exploitation

- Using your kindness, time, money, or labor for personal gain.
- Often cloaked in appeals for help or loyalty.

11. 😱 Fear Mongering

- Intimidation or exaggerated risks used to coerce you into a decision or action.
- Common in toxic workplaces or emotionally volatile relationships.

12. 🎭 Playing the Victim

- Avoiding accountability by flipping the script and painting themselves as the wronged party.
- Exploits your compassion and keeps you defending or rescuing them.

13. ⏮️ Reverse Psychology

- Suggesting the opposite of what they want in order to provoke a reaction.
- Plays on autonomy and a desire to assert independence.

🧠 EMOTIONAL TRIGGERS: THE MANIPULATOR'S FUEL

Emotional triggers are past experiences or traumas that cause disproportionate emotional reactions in the present. Manipulators expertly identify these triggers—fear of abandonment, guilt, insecurity, or rejection—and exploit them to keep you reactive, confused, and off-balance.

- **Examples:**
  - Childhood abandonment triggers panic when someone doesn't reply quickly.
  - Past trauma that occurred during the holidays can make it a time of emotional vulnerability.
  - Guilt over not helping someone enough is used to coerce you into compliance.

👉 *Recognizing your own triggers is the first step in disarming manipulative influence.*

🧛 EMOTIONAL VAMPIRES

These people drain your emotional energy and leave you feeling exhausted, insecure, or anxious. Common types include:

- **The Controller** – Must be in charge of everything.
- **The Fake Positivity Person** – Dismisses your real struggles.
- **The Narcissist** – Demands admiration, offers none.
- **The One-Upper** – Constantly competes for the spotlight.
- **The Victim** – Perpetually oppressed, never empowered.
- **The Constant Talker** – Drains energy with self-focused monologues.
- **The Drama Queen** – Lives in chaos, thrives on crisis.

How to Defend Yourself:

- Set boundaries.
- Limit time and energy investment.
- Practice assertive communication.
- Avoid taking emotional bait or rescuing them.

⚖️ POWER DYNAMICS: THE HIDDEN ENGINE OF MANIPULATION

Power imbalances drive most emotional manipulation. The dominant partner (romantic or professional) may wield control through fear, guilt, obligation, or reward.

💪 **Types of Power:**

- **Coercive Power** – Control through threats and punishment.
- **Legitimate Power** – Authority from recognized roles (e.g., parent, boss).
- **Expert Power** – Influence through specialized knowledge.

👉 *Understanding who holds power, how they use it, and how it affects your responses is key to reclaiming autonomy.*

🧘 EMOTIONAL DEFENSE: YOUR PROTECTION TOOLKIT

🛠️ **Tools to Protect Yourself:**

1. 🌱 **Mindfulness**

- Stay present and observe emotions without judgment.
- Reduces impulsive reactions and creates space for intentional responses.

2. 🖼️ **Cognitive Reframing**

- Change the way you interpret manipulation attempts.
- "This guilt is not my responsibility" vs. "I must make them happy."

3. 🏃 Assertive Boundaries

- Learn to say no without guilt.
- Be firm, clear, and consistent.

4. 🎗 Support System

- Stay connected to trusted friends, family, or professionals.
- Helps you reality-check and avoid isolation.

5. ⚡ Energy Inventory

- Notice how you feel after interactions.
- Prioritize relationships that energize, not drain.

🎯 Bullseye Recap

✅ Core Manipulation Tactics

- Gaslighting
- Guilt Tripping
- Silent Treatment
- Exploitation
- Emotional Blackmail
- Reverse Psychology
- Playing the Victim
- Triangulation
- Fear Mongering
- Love Bombing

✅ **Signs You're Being Manipulated**

- You're questioning your reality.
- You feel obligated or guilty ... often.
- Your confidence and independence are eroding.
- You feel isolated or constantly confused.
- You're drained after certain interactions.

✅ **Tools for Defense**

- Self-awareness of your emotional triggers.
- Clear, assertive boundaries.
- Mindfulness and grounding practices.
- Reframing tactics and emotional detachment.
- Limit exposure to emotional vampires.
- Build supportive, affirming connections.

💥 _The Quick & Dirty_

1. Manipulators use your empathy and emotions against you—not because you're weak, but because you're kind.

2. Emotional triggers are entry points for control. Learn them, own them, protect them.

3. The most common tactics (gaslighting, guilt, blackmail) often feel subtle or confusing—by design.

4. Power dynamics are central to manipulation. Identify them to rebalance control.

5. You are allowed to protect your peace. Saying no, walking away, or standing up for yourself isn't mean—it's healthy.

6. Self-care, boundaries, and emotional intelligence are your shield. They reduce your vulnerability and help you reclaim agency.

CHAPTER 6
COVERT INFLUENCE AND DARK PERSUASION TACTICS

" *"Manipulation is the dark side of charisma."*

~ Max Weber

Hey, LMK the chapter summary for "Covert Influence and Dark Persuasion Tactics." 🤩 I'm curious & I gotta know!

NP, manipulation doesn't always shout—it often whispers. This chapter unveils the subtle art of covert influence, where manipulation is disguised as concern, charisma, or helpfulness. These tactics often leave you second-guessing yourself without ever realizing you've been influenced. Whether it's a passive-aggressive colleague, an overly helpful friend with strings attached, or a marketing campaign triggering FOMO 😰 the goal is the same: control.

From **covert aggression** to **reciprocity**, **social proof**, and even **psychological warfare**, this chapter exposes how manipulators plant seeds of doubt, shape behavior, and secure compliance—all while keeping their hands clean. The key to resisting this form of dark persuasion lies in awareness, boundary-setting, and reclaiming agency.

🕵️ COVERT AGGRESSION: SILENT CONTROL

Covert aggressors are **manipulative but indirect**. Instead of confronting you head-on, they employ:

- **Sarcastic Jabs**
- **Backhanded Compliments**
- **Emotional Withdrawal**
- **Feigned Ignorance**

⭐ These tactics undermine your confidence and create a dynamic where you chase their validation. They're driven by **insecurity masked as control**, relying on ambiguity and passive-aggression to destabilize your footing while maintaining their false appearance of innocence.

🌱 **Reflection Prompt:** Journal moments that made you feel "off" after interactions. Covert tactics often feel like something is wrong—but you can't pinpoint what.

🎁 MANIPULATIVE HELPFULNESS: CONTROL IN DISGUISE

Some manipulators **weaponize generosity:**

- They offer unsolicited help to create dependency.
- They use past favors as guilt leverage.
- They condition their "support" on future obligations.

This so-called helpfulness chips away at your autonomy. You might feel incapable of making your own decisions and feel guilty for rejecting help—even if it's unwelcome.

👉 *Defense: Respond with, "Thanks, I've got this," and establish boundaries without guilt. Kindness isn't an IOU.*

🔁 RECIPROCITY: "YOU OWE ME"

The principle of reciprocity is rooted in human psychology: when someone gives to us, we feel compelled to give back. Manipulators exploit this by:

- Giving gifts or favors strategically
- Expecting immediate or disproportionate returns
- Using guilt to enforce payback

In marketing, freebies, samples, and gestures of goodwill often push consumers toward purchase. Politicians and fundraisers use this principle to secure loyalty and donations.

👉 *Defense: Appreciate the gesture but assess if it's tied to expectation. You're allowed to say "thank you" without obligating yourself.*

🔗 COMMITMENT & CONSISTENCY: THE PSYCHOLOGY OF AGREEMENT

Once we make a choice—especially publicly—we want to stay consistent with it. Manipulators exploit this via:

- **Foot-in-the-Door Techniques** (small asks leading to big ones)
- **Sunk Cost Fallacy** (you stick with bad decisions because of prior investment)
- **Verbal Commitments** that prime you for larger actions

This drive to remain consistent can trap you in relationships, jobs, or decisions that no longer serve you.

👉 *Defense: Ask yourself, "Would I say yes to this today if I weren't already invested?"*

👥 SOCIAL PROOF: FOLLOWING THE CROWD

People tend to do what others are doing—especially under uncertainty. Social proof appears as:

- Glowing online reviews
- Celebrity endorsements
- "Everyone is doing it" messaging

This herd mentality influences both buying behavior and decision-making within teams or communities. It fosters conformity and suppresses dissent.

👉 *Defense: Ask yourself, "Am I making this decision based on what I want —or because others are doing it?"*

⌛ SCARCITY: THE ILLUSION OF URGENCY

We value things more when they're rare or limited. Scarcity triggers:

- FOMO (fear of missing out)
- Panic buying
- Rash decisions under pressure

Sales tactics like countdown timers, "only 3 left!" alerts, and exclusive memberships manipulate this instinct to nudge you toward impulsive behavior.

👉 *Defense: Pause. Breathe. Ask, "Would I want this if it were freely available?"*

🗡 PSYCHOLOGICAL WARFARE: THE WEAPONIZED MIND

This form of dark persuasion includes:

- **Demoralization** – undermining confidence through subtle criticism
- **Propaganda** – using biased or false information to sway public opinion
- **False Flag Operations** – deceiving audiences by misattributing responsibility
- **Fear-Based Messaging** – manipulating behavior through threats or doom scenarios
- **Influence Operations** – gradual, subtle changes to shift group attitudes

These tactics are used in media, politics, and even personal relationships to manufacture doubt, fear, or division.

👉 *Defense: Be a critical thinker. Fact-check. Ask who benefits from your belief or behavior.*

🎯 **Bullseye Recap**

✅ **Covert Influence Tactics**

- **Sarcasm, withdrawal, passive-aggression** = covert aggression
- **"Helpful" people** who use favors as control = manipulative helpfulness
- **Guilt-laden generosity** = weaponized reciprocity
- **Commitment traps** = sunk cost fallacy + verbal agreements
- **Following the crowd** = social proof manipulation
- **Limited-time offers** = scarcity plays on urgency and FOMO
- **Media/political manipulation** = psychological warfare and propaganda

---

☀ The Quick & Dirty

1. Covert manipulation often leaves you doubting yourself. Trust your gut—confusion is often the first sign.

2. Manipulators hide control behind generosity. If help comes with strings, it's not help—it's bait.

3. Reciprocity is a powerful influence lever. You can receive without repaying.

4. Commitment can trap you. Consistency is admirable—blind loyalty is not.

5. Social proof shapes groupthink. Be mindful of where your values end and group pressure begins.

6. Scarcity manipulates urgency. Delay your decision to reclaim power.

7. Psychological warfare is real. Guard your beliefs like valuables; propaganda thrives on blind trust.

8. Awareness is your superpower. Once you see these tactics, they lose much of their power.

CHAPTER 7
ADVANCED MIND CONTROL TECHNI

> "*The best way to manipulate a man is to make him think he is manipulating you.*"
>
> ~ John Smith

Hey, what's the chapter summary for "Advanced Mind Control Techniques"? TBH I think I need to know this! 🪄

Well, IRL mind control is often misunderstood as dramatic hypnosis or overt manipulation. In reality, it's much subtler—BOLO because it's woven into marketing, politics, and everyday social interaction. This chapter peels back the curtain on how mind control tactics shape our decisions through authority, suggestion, anchoring, cognitive bias, and more. 🤯

These techniques don't force us—they **guide, prime, and persuade**, often without us realizing it. Whether through the charm of an authority figure, the precision of framing a message, or the strategic use of emotional triggers, these tools influence behavior by exploiting how the human brain shortcuts decision-making.

👉 *The good news? Once you recognize these techniques, you can build your immunity to manipulation—and even use some of them ethically to influence and empower yourself or others.*

🔑 KEY TECHNIQUES & CONCEPTS

💼 Authority

- People tend to obey figures who appear knowledgeable, credible, or prestigious.
- Lab coats, titles, uniforms, and perceived expertise trigger automatic trust.
- Often used in advertising, politics, and negotiation to elicit compliance.

👉 *Defense: Ask yourself, "Is this authority legitimate, or am I outsourcing my thinking?"*

⚓ Anchoring

- The **first piece of information** we receive creates a mental reference point.
- Used in pricing, negotiations, and first impressions to shape judgments.
- Also linked to emotional anchoring (e.g., using music, scent, or settings to trigger feelings).

👉 *Application: Set a positive tone early in interactions; be mindful of initial impressions.*

🧠 **Cognitive Biases**

Mental shortcuts used by the brain that often lead to faulty reasoning.

- **Confirmation Bias** – You favor info that confirms what you already believe.
- **Anchoring Bias** – You rely too much on initial info when making decisions.
- **Availability Heuristic** – You overestimate what's most memorable or recent.
- **Hindsight Bias** – You believe you "knew it all along" after an event occurs.
- **Attribution Bias** – You judge others harshly while excusing your own behavior.
- **Scarcity Bias** – You assign more value to things that seem rare or exclusive.

👉 *Defense: Slow down your thinking. Ask yourself, "Am I reacting out of instinct, fear, or bias?"*

⚖️ Cognitive Dissonance

- When beliefs and actions conflict, we experience discomfort —and we change one to resolve it.
- Manipulators use this to nudge behavior: show inconsistency, and let discomfort motivate change.

Marketing Example: "If you care about the environment, why don't you drive this hybrid?"

👉 *Defense: Be mindful of emotional discomfort used to trigger compliance. Align actions with values—not guilt.*

🧩 FRAMING

- How something is **presented** affects how we interpret it.
- "90% fat-free" sounds healthier than "10% fat."
- Framing can make the same facts feel hopeful or hopeless, exciting or threatening.

👉 *Application: Use framing to encourage optimism and confidence in self-talk or leadership.*

🧠 PRIMING

- Exposure to specific stimuli **primes** you to behave or think a certain way.
- Visuals, sounds, words, and smells can all shape your mood or choices.
- Often used in branding, environments, or communication for subtle influence.

👉 *Defense: Tune in to your surroundings. Ask yourself "Is my mood or reaction being nudged?"*

🟫 INFLUENCE TACTICS: FOOT-IN-THE-DOOR & DOOR-IN-THE-FACE

- **Foot-in-the-Door:** Get agreement on something small to increase compliance with something larger.
- **Door-in-the-Face:** Ask for something big first (expecting a no), then retreat to the real, smaller request.

👉 *Application: Great for sales, persuasion, and negotiation—but ethically, please.*

💬 THE POWER OF SUGGESTION

- Influencing ideas by planting subtle, emotional, or visual cues.
- Effective suggestion uses **language patterns**, **imagery**, and **confidence** to shift behavior.

👉 *Example: "Imagine how confident you'll feel after your presentation." (Encourages visualization and action.)*

💪 SELF-DEVELOPMENT WITH MIND CONTROL TOOLS

These techniques aren't just for dodging manipulation—they're also powerful tools for **growth and motivation**.

- **Set Goals:** Break large goals into small wins that build momentum.
- **Positive Self-Talk:** Reframe inner dialogue to support growth.
- **Visualization:** Mentally rehearse success; use all senses to strengthen belief.
- **Journaling:** Track behaviors, triggers, and progress for self-awareness.
- **Reframe Failures:** Instead of "I failed," say "I learned."

👉 *You can prime your day, re-anchor your habits, and use subtle mental framing to shift how you see challenges—from threats into opportunities.*

🎯 **Bullseye Recap**

✅ **Covert Mind Control Techniques**

- **Authority:** Obedience to experts or titles.
- **Anchoring:** First impressions or prices set expectations.
- **Cognitive Biases:** Flawed mental shortcuts that cloud judgment.
- **Cognitive Dissonance:** Discomfort between beliefs and actions prompts change.
- **Framing:** Recasting facts to control perception.
- **Priming:** Environmental cues shape behavior subconsciously.
- **Foot-in-the-Door:** Small ask → big ask.
- **Door-in-the-Face:** Big ask → real ask.
- **Suggestion:** Language + imagery = subtle persuasion.

💥 _The Quick & Dirty_

1. Mind control is subtle influence, not sci-fi. It thrives in everyday decisions.

2. Awareness is defense. When you know how you're being influenced, you're less likely to fall for it.

3. Anchors, biases, and frames shape your perception and decisions without your full awareness.

4. You can use these techniques ethically to motivate, influence, and grow.

5. Suggestion is powerful—choose your words, imagery, and inner dialogue wisely.

6. Manipulators are skilled in exploiting weakness—you must be skilled in spotting it.

7. Turn manipulation into empowerment by applying these tools to your goals and mental resilience.

CHAPTER 8

HARNESSING ADVANCED TECHNIQUES IN HYPNOSIS WITH NLP

> " *When words are used to conceal rather than reveal, they cease to be tools of communication and become weapons of control.*"
>
> ~ *Unknown*

Hey, what's the chapter summary for Harnessing Advanced Techniques in Hypnosis with NLP? 🫨 Just trying to do my DD!

Hey there! GMTA … This chapter dives into the powerful, misunderstood world of hypnosis and Neuro-Linguistic Programming (NLP)—not as parlor tricks or mystical arts, but as influential psychological tools that shape behavior, promote transformation, and, yes, carry the potential for manipulation if misused.🙂

Hypnosis and NLP work by bypassing the conscious mind to speak directly to the subconscious—the seat of habit, emotion, and memory. Through storytelling, symbolism, pacing, and suggestion, practitioners can instill change, build trust, influence behavior, and rewrite old narratives. When used ethically, these tools can support self-healing, goal achievement, communication mastery, and emotional freedom.

🐙 HYPNOSIS: FROM SHAMANS TO SELF-DISCOVERY

- **Origins:** Traced from ancient shamans to 18th-century "animal magnetism" (Franz Mesmer) to wartime propaganda and modern therapeutic tools.
- **Modern Use:** Hypnosis is now used for stress reduction, habit change (e.g., smoking, eating, phobias), and emotional healing.
- **Trance State:** Not mind control—it's a state of heightened focus and relaxation that makes the subconscious more receptive to suggestions.
- **Suggestibility:** Language patterns are key. Positive suggestions can reinforce growth; negative ones can do damage.

👉 *Reflection Exercise: Consider moments when you felt unusually receptive to someone's words. What triggered it?*

💬 CONVERSATIONAL HYPNOSIS: INFLUENCE WITHOUT FORMAL TRANCE

Hypnosis doesn't require a swinging watch—it can happen through **everyday conversation.**

- **Conversational hypnosis** is about guiding attention, building rapport, and delivering subtle suggestions while the listener is relaxed and unaware.

🥘 RECIPE FOR CONVERSATIONAL HYPNOSIS

1. 👯 Build Rapport

- Use pacing (mirroring), leading, and deep listening.
- Speak in their language (emotional, logical, sensory).
- Establish trust before attempting to guide.

2. 🐿️ Distract the Conscious Mind

- Overload the rational brain with stories, rhythm, metaphors.
- Use rhythmic speech, tone changes, complex or contradictory language to induce light trance.

3. 📦 Deliver Embedded Suggestions

- "Wouldn't it be nice to feel confident now?"
- Weave commands into casual phrasing, stories, or metaphors.
- Use soft suggestions first, then escalate.

👉 *Defense Against It: Watch for shifts in tone, long run-on sentences, or disorienting metaphors. Stay mentally grounded.*

🧠 NLP (NEURO-LINGUISTIC PROGRAMMING): THE USER MANUAL FOR YOUR BRAIN

💡 Core Concepts

- Developed in the 1970s to model the success of top therapists like Milton Erickson.
- Focuses on how language and thought influence behavior.

🔑 Key Components

- **Representation Systems:** We process reality through visual, auditory, and kinesthetic filters.
- **Modeling:** Copying successful thought patterns or behaviors of others.
- **Mirroring:** Matching someone's body language or speech to build rapport and trust.

👉 *Pro Tip: "I see what you mean" for visuals, "That rings a bell" for auditory, "That feels right" for kinesthetic.*

🔄 NLP TECHNIQUES FOR INFLUENCE & CHANGE

⚓ Anchoring

- Link emotions to a stimulus (song, touch, word).
- Can be used to boost confidence, reduce fear, or influence others in subtle ways.

🎧 Embedded Commands

- Sneak commands into natural speech to bypass conscious resistance.

👉 *Example: "You might find yourself feeling more energized now.*

🌀 Submodalities

- Change how a memory is encoded (color, size, distance) to shift the emotional response.
- Diminish fear or amplify motivation.

✨ The Swish Pattern

- Replace negative imagery with a strong, motivating visual using a "mental snap."
- Great for breaking habits like procrastination or anxiety spirals.

⏳ Timeline Therapy

- Travel through your mental history to reframe traumatic or limiting memories.
- Offers emotional release and new perspectives.

🧍 NLP IN REAL LIFE

- **Sales:** Tailor pitches based on a client's meta-programs (detail vs. big-picture thinkers).
- **Leadership:** Motivate teams based on how they internally represent challenges.
- **Therapy:** Clear phobias, reframe identity, and enhance self-awareness.
- **Self-Hypnosis** Use affirmations, journaling, and visualization to rewire beliefs.

⚠️ *Warning: NLP has critics. Though many find it transformative, scientific evidence is limited. Ethical practice is key.*

🎯 **Bullseye Recap**

✅ **Hypnosis Essentials**

- Uses trance to bypass conscious resistance.
- Enhances focus, reduces stress, transforms behavior.
- Language = the delivery system for change.

✅ **Conversational Hypnosis**

- Everyday dialogue = opportunity for subtle influence.
- Rapport, distraction, and suggestion = hypnotic trifecta.
- Ethical responsibility is essential.

✅ **NLP Techniques**

- **Anchoring:** Link emotions to cues.

- **Embedded Commands:** Suggest change through subtle language.
- **Submodalities:** Change perception, change feelings.
- **Swish Pattern:** Swap fear for empowerment.
- **Timeline Therapy:** Reframe the past to heal the present.

☀ The Quick & Dirty

1. Hypnosis is not control—it's permission. It opens the subconscious to influence, not domination.

2. Conversational hypnosis works because it feels natural. Trust and subtle suggestion are its foundations.

3. NLP is a toolkit for understanding and influencing thought. But it must be used ethically.

4. Your subconscious is trainable. Through anchors, metaphors, and reframing, you can shape your habits and beliefs.

5. These techniques can heal, transform, or manipulate. The intention determines the impact.

6. Always vet who you allow to "program" your mind. Not everyone has your best interests in mind.

7. Mastering these tools is mastering yourself. Use them to build confidence, clarity, and courage.

CHAPTER 9

NAVIGATING PROFESSIONAL ENVIRONMENTS WITH DARK PSYCHOLOGY

> *"The art of manipulation lies in the ability to make others feel empowered while quietly pulling the strings."*
>
> *~ Unknown*

Hey! What's the DL for "Navigating Professional Environments with Dark Psychology"? 🧑‍💼

Hi! So, IMHO the workplace isn't just about to-do lists, coffee ☕ breaks, and chasing KPIs—it's a real-life chessboard where power, influence, and manipulation often play out beneath the surface. This chapter arms you with the skills to thrive in complex professional environments using principles of dark psychology, not to exploit, but to defend, influence ethically, and lead effectively.

75

Y ou'll explore how to command a persuasive leadership presence, apply psychological tactics in negotiation, and decode the behavior of manipulative colleagues—all while keeping your integrity intact. By integrating emotional intelligence, subtle influence, and ethical persuasion, you'll sharpen your edge without crossing moral lines.

🎯 LEADERSHIP & INFLUENCE: BUILDING A PERSUASIVE PRESENCE

🔖 Key Concepts:

- Leadership isn't just authority—it's **vision, empathy, and influence.**
- **Storytelling** is a superpower. Use it to connect, inspire, and convey complex ideas with clarity.
- **Empathy + Assertiveness** = Magnetic Leadership. Listen deeply and motivate through respect.
- **Recognition** and **constructive feedback** build trust and motivation.
- Blend **transformational leadership** (vision and inspiration) with **transactional leadership** (structure and rewards) to suit different needs.
- **Emotional intelligence (EI)** is essential—especially in conflict, crisis, or team dynamics.

📓 Practical Leadership Strategies:

- Attend leadership workshops to grow skills like communication, feedback, and team-building.
- Conduct self-assessments to pinpoint areas for growth.

- Prioritize active listening and team morale.
- Use emotional regulation to stay composed under pressure.

👏 NEGOTIATION TACTICS: PSYCHOLOGY MEETS STRATEGY

Negotiation isn't war—it's persuasion with structure. Understanding the psychological levers that guide behavior gives you a major advantage.

🛠 Tactical Tools:

- **Reciprocity:** Offer a small concession first to inspire a return gesture.
- **Scarcity:** Highlight urgency or limited availability to create perceived value.
- **Anchoring:** Set the first price or offer to shape the reference point for the rest of the negotiation.
- **Framing:** Present your proposal positively (e.g., "investment" vs. "cost") to shift perception.

💻 Effective Prep:

- Research the other party's needs, goals, and objections.
- Rehearse your points and visualize ideal outcomes.
- Use open-ended questions to uncover deeper motives.
- Stay transparent and aim for win-win outcomes.

💪 **Power Tip:** *Ethics build trust. Strategic transparency makes you look strong and trustworthy—two key traits for long-term influence.*

🐢 MANAGING MANIPULATIVE COLLEAGUES

Recognizing the Behavior:

- **Passive-Aggression:** Subtle digs, backhanded compliments, and sarcasm.
- **Withholding Info:** Excluding you from key meetings or "forgetting" to CC you.
- **Credit Theft:** Taking your ideas and presenting them as their own.
- **Gatekeeping:** Hoarding information to maintain power.
- **Triangulation & Gossip:** Spreading rumors, pitting coworkers against each other.

💥 Impact:

- Erodes trust and team morale.
- Damages collaboration, creativity, and innovation.
- Can lead to burnout, anxiety, and disengagement.

🛡 Defensive Strategies:

- **Stay Calm:** Don't let emotional responses derail you.
- **Call It Out Professionally:** Address behavior, not character.
- **Document Interactions:** Keep email trails and meeting notes.
- **Build Alliances:** Develop trusted allies and peer support.
- **Escalate Wisely:** Know when to bring in HR or leadership.

‼️ *Bottom Line: Maintain boundaries. Manipulators thrive on your silence —don't give them that luxury.*

🎯 **Bullseye Recap**

✅ **Leadership**

- Persuasion > Authority.
- Use stories, empathy, and energy to inspire.
- Emotional intelligence is your anchor.

✅ **Negotiation**

- **Reciprocity:** Give to get.
- **Scarcity:** Use urgency to inspire action.
- **Anchoring:** Set the tone early.
- **Framing:** Package the offer to shape perception.
- **Preparation and ethics = influence and trust.**

✅ **Office Manipulators**

- Watch for passive-aggression, exclusion, and credit theft.
- Stay grounded and respond with facts.
- Build support, document everything, and escalate if necessary.

💥 *The Quick & Dirty*

1. Leadership is influence with empathy. People follow those who inspire, listen, and support—not just those who bark orders.

2. Psychological tactics enhance negotiations. Anchoring, scarcity, and framing are tools—not tricks—when used ethically.

3. Manipulation is often subtle. Pay attention to patterns and protect your emotional space.

4. Emotional intelligence sets you apart. In chaos, calm is your superpower.

5. Trust is your best currency. Whether in leadership or negotiation, integrity creates loyalty and cooperation.

6. Self-awareness and preparation win battles. Know your goals, know your opposition, and always be ready to adapt.

7. Boundaries matter. You can't control manipulators—but you can control your responses.

CHAPTER 10
SOCIAL MEDIA MANIPULATION PROTECTING DIGITAL PRESENCE

> *"Everyone sees what you appear to be, few experience what you really are."*
>
> ~ Niccolò Machiavelli, *The Prince*

Hey! What's the 📖 chapter summary for "Social Media Manipulation & Protecting Digital Presence"? JW 🐞

Well, FWIW, welcome to the era where your phone 📱 knows your fears, cravings, and secret obsessions—and uses them against you with algorithmic precision. Social media platforms, powered by invisible algorithms and data-hungry tech, act like digital puppeteers, subtly manipulating what you see, believe, and even buy. This chapter exposes the tactics used to control online experiences, shape public opinion, and influence your behaviors, often without your awareness. SMH, I know.

With emotionally charged headlines, curated influencer feeds, and targeted ads tailored to your digital fingerprint, social media creates a distorted version of reality. Recognizing these manipulation techniques is the first step in reclaiming your autonomy in the digital world.

📌 KEY CONCEPTS

🔍 Algorithmic Control

- Algorithms curate your feed based on what captures your attention (likes, clicks, pauses).
- Content is prioritized not by truth or balance, but by **engagement potential.**
- **"PRIME"** content—Prestigious, In-group, Moral, and Emotional—is most amplified.
- The result: echo chambers, viral misinformation, and distorted realities.

⚠️ The Illusion of Choice

- You're not choosing what to see—algorithms already filtered it.
- High-engagement content dominates your feed, regardless of its accuracy.
- Fake news spreads faster than facts because it is **designed to provoke emotion.**

TYPES OF DIGITAL MANIPULATION

Influencer Persuasion

- Influencers blend authenticity with advertising, often without disclosure.
- Recommendations feel personal but may be sponsored or scripted.
- Influencers shape behavior around health, beauty, politics, and lifestyle—sometimes irresponsibly.

Psychological Impact

- **Comparison Trap:** Polished highlight reels increase anxiety and reduce self-esteem.
- **Information Overload:** Conflicting messages cause confusion, fear, and apathy.
- **Echo Chambers:** Repeated exposure to similar content reinforces bias and discourages critical thought.

Targeted Ads & Behavioral Nudging

- Ads are tailored to your online behavior, emotional state, and preferences.
- This can affect purchases, opinions, political leanings, and identity.
- Manipulation feels like personalization—but it's designed to benefit advertisers, not you.

PRACTICAL TOOLS FOR PROTECTION

Media Literacy

- **Evaluate Sources:** Who's behind the message? What's their agenda?
- **Spot Red Flags:** Sensational headlines, emotionally charged language, lack of citation.
- **Check Credibility:** Use fact-checkers like Snopes, PolitiFact, or Media Bias/Fact Check.

👑 Spotting Bots & Fake Accounts

- Generic names, low engagement, repeated content = likely bot behavior.
- Bots post excessively, lack personal content, and mimic human patterns poorly.
- Fake engagement (likes, comments) can create the illusion of popularity and credibility.

🔐 Privacy & Awareness

- Adjust privacy settings: Limit data sharing, ad targeting, and app access.
- Don't overshare personal info that can be used to target or manipulate you.
- Cross-reference news before sharing and take note of manipulative timing (e.g., content released during emotional or controversial events).

📝 DIGITAL AWARENESS & DETOX

👉 **Reflection Exercise: Create a "Digital Awareness Journal"**

- Track your social media habits for one week. For posts that stir strong emotions:
  - What was the post about?

- o How did it make you feel?
- o Why did it resonate with you?
- o Did you share or comment? Why?
- o Does it align with your values?

🧘 Try a Digital Detox

- Step away from platforms temporarily.
- Notice your mindset, focus, and emotional state without social media noise.
- Return with clearer boundaries and intentional habits.

🚩 HOW TO IDENTIFY MANIPULATION ONLINE

🤟 Language & Tone

- Emotional appeals and urgency bypass rational thinking.
- "You won't believe this!" and "Everyone's talking about it!" are clickbait signals.
- Be wary of moral outrage or anything that triggers extreme reactions.

⏰ Timing & Virality

- Manipulative posts often appear during emotionally charged events to influence public perception.
- Viral misinformation outpaces corrections—emotion drives faster sharing than truth.

⛳ Engagement Red Flags

- Generic comments like "Love this!" or "Great!" may signal bot-generated engagement.

- Disproportionate likes/followers to comment ratios = suspicious activity.

💰 Follow the Money (or Influence)

- Who benefits if you believe this message?
- Influencer posts may be backed by sponsorships or political agendas.
- Transparency is key—lack of it should spark skepticism.

✏️ REAL-WORLD EXAMPLES

ℹ️ Viral Misinformation

- False health remedies or exaggerated political claims get mass exposure.
- Emotional hooks (fear, outrage, hope) override rational assessment.
- Once embedded, falsehoods persist even after corrections—creating long-term confusion and skepticism.

🔍 Influencer Campaigns

- Influencers drive purchases by appearing "relatable."
- Trust builds quickly—even when promotion is disguised as personal endorsement.
- Lack of disclosure can mislead audiences and lead to poor decisions or regret.

◉ BULLET POINT RECAP

Digital Literacy Companion Checklist

Use this checklist to help clients, students, or team members navigate social media with awareness and protect their digital presence.

✅ **1. Spotting Manipulation in Your Feed**

- Is the post using emotionally charged language (fear, outrage, extreme excitement)?
- Does the headline feel too shocking or "clickbait-ish" to be real?
- Are you seeing only one perspective repeatedly (possible echo chamber)?
- Have you fact-checked the post using reputable sources?

✅ **2. Verifying Content & Sources**

- Can you identify the original source of the post or article?
- Is the author credible or an expert in the topic?
- Does the post cite evidence, data, or trustworthy references?
- Does the post link to reputable news organizations or fact-checkers?

✅ **3. Recognizing Bots & Fake Accounts**

- Does the account have a real photo and personal information?
- Are comments generic or repeated across other posts ("Nice post!," "So true!")?
- Is the account posting 24/7 with unusually high frequency?
- Is the follower-to-engagement ratio suspiciously off (e.g., 10K followers but 2 likes)?

✅ **4. Strengthening Digital Hygiene**

- Are your privacy settings updated across all social platforms?
- Do you limit how much personal information you share online?
- Do you avoid clicking suspicious or emotionally manipulative links?
- Have you taken a recent break (digital detox) to evaluate your screen time?

✅ 5. Mindful Media Habits

- Do you reflect before commenting, sharing, or reacting emotionally?
- Are you diversifying your content sources (left, right, center, global)?
- Do you journal or track your emotional responses to posts that trigger you?
- Are you helping others recognize manipulation by modeling thoughtful engagement?

☀ The Quick & Dirty

1. You are not fully in control of your feed. Algorithms decide what you see based on your data and predicted emotional triggers.

2. Fake news thrives on emotion. If something makes you angry, scared, or thrilled—pause before sharing.

3. Influencers influence more than products. Their opinions shape behaviors, beliefs, and even identity.

4. Privacy isn't automatic. Regularly audit your settings, apps, and what you're giving away for free.

5. Critical thinking is your armor. Don't accept posts at face value—question, research, verify.

6. Bots and fake accounts are everywhere. Learn to spot patterns and avoid being drawn into engineered conversations.

7. Digital literacy is essential. Educate yourself and others on how to consume information consciously.

8. Your mental health matters. Curated feeds can harm self-esteem. Detox, reflect, and set mindful screen boundaries.

CHAPTER 11
PRACTICAL APPLICATIONS AND REAL-WORLD SCENARIOS

> " *"Control thrives where awareness fails—manipulation isn't power taken, but influence given."*
>
> ~ Wynne Wick

Hey! JW What's the chapter summary for "Practical Applications and Real-World Scenarios"? 🌎 EILI5

Hi! TW - the lowdown on this chapter is that it uncovers the sophisticated ways dark psychology techniques manifest across modern society. From emotionally charged political campaigns to the magnetic pull of celebrity culture, this section highlights how psychological influence operates in ⏰ real time—and how to stay sharp, skeptical, and empowered. JSYK, my friend.

🧊 POLITICAL PERSUASION

ore Idea: Politicians use emotional appeals to build connection, motivate action, and reinforce belief systems.

- Repetition and slogans become mental anchors ("Hope and Change," "Make America Great Again").
- Iconic speeches use emotion, vivid imagery, and rhythm to stir collective consciousness.
- Digital strategies now blend data analytics, behavioral targeting, and emotion-driven messaging.

🎓 Ethical Dilemma: Is it ethical to use fear or outrage to win votes?

💥 Impact: Emotional messaging can deepen division, polarize groups, and create echo chambers.

👉 *Takeaway: Awareness of emotional manipulation in politics allows you to make more objective decisions.*

💼 MARKETING MANIPULATION

Core Idea: Marketing doesn't just sell products—it engineers desire using psychological triggers.

- **Scarcity:** "Only 3 left in stock!" creates urgency (FOMO).
- **Social Proof:** "Everyone's buying this!" leads you to jump on the bandwagon.
- **Emotional Branding:** Storytelling connects emotionally and embeds brand loyalty.

- **Anchoring:** High initial price tags make sales seem like deals.
- **Design Psychology:** Sleek interfaces and nostalgic symbols trigger emotional and aesthetic appeal.

🌏 **Real-World Tactic:** Loyalty programs leverage consistency to encourage repeat buying.

👉 *Takeaway: The next time you're "sold," stop and ask yourself—was it your choice or theirs?*

🕵️ CULT TACTICS & GROUP CONTROL

Core Idea: Cults and cult-like groups exploit psychological needs—belonging, identity, certainty—to exert deep control.

- **Gradual indoctrination** and emotional rewards replace critical thinking.
- **Isolation** from external influences creates dependency on the group.
- Leaders position themselves as saviors or sole truth-bearers.
- Modern equivalents exist in politics, business, and wellness communities.

📓 **Real World Case Examples:**

- Jim Jones used charisma and seclusion to dismantle personal autonomy.
- David Koresh manipulated his following with emotional fervor and "divine" authority.

👉 *Takeaway: Any group that discourages outside input or absolute loyalty should raise red flags.*

⭐ CELEBRITY INFLUENCE

Core Idea: Celebrities shape beliefs, trends, and consumer behavior through parasocial relationships (one-sided emotional bonds).

- **Influencer Economy:** Endorsements feel personal, but often are scripted, sponsored, and psychologically targeted.
- **Identity Projection:** Fans buy into products not for utility, but to emulate the celebrity's persona.
- **Emotional Connection:** Authentic-seeming content feels trustworthy—whether it is or not.
- **Trendsetting:** Stars can launch fashion trends, wellness fads, or lifestyle shifts overnight.

🌐 **Real World Case Examples**

- Meghan Markle's outfits sell out in hours.
- Leonardo DiCaprio's climate advocacy mobilizes eco-conscious action.
- Rihanna and The Rock leverage personal branding to launch massively successful companies.

👉 *Takeaway: Don't confuse admiration with credibility—evaluate both the product and the promoter.*

🏃 PSYCHOLOGICAL WARFARE IN COMPETITIVE SPACES

🔲 **Core Idea:** In business, sports, and personal rivalries, manipulation often hides under the guise of "strategy."

- **Mental Intimidation:** Confident body language, verbal jabs, and timing are used to rattle opponents.
- **Pre-Performance Mind Games:** Athletes and leaders use visual dominance, rehearsed confidence, and calculated distractions.
- **Rivalries:** Apple vs. Samsung, Federer vs. Nadal—winning includes controlling narrative and perception.

🎓 **Ethical Considerations:**

- When does confidence become coercion?
- Should manipulation for performance gains be acceptable?

👉 *Takeaway: True power is remaining composed under psychological fire —practice mindfulness and ethical assertiveness.*

◯ **Reflection Prompts**

Use these for journaling or discussion:

- What emotional appeals have shaped your decisions recently?
- Have you ever joined a group (or fandom) that later felt manipulative?

- How do you feel after a shopping spree—empowered or emotionally "played"?
- Which celebrity's values align with your own? Do their endorsements still hold up?
- Have you ever used mental tactics to get your way? Were they ethical?

👉 *This chapter pulled back the curtain on manipulation across industries and environments. From inspiring speeches to curated celebrity posts, influence is everywhere—but so is your ability to resist it.* 💪

🎯 BULLSEYE RECAP: TOOLS FOR REAL-WORLD DEFENSE

✅ **Recognize Emotional Triggers:** Ask yourself—"What am I being made to feel? Why?"

✅ **Question Familiarity:** If something feels "natural" or "obvious," you may have been primed.

✅ **Avoid Auto-Pilot Thinking:** Pause before you act—especially in politics, purchasing, or group settings.

✅ **Set Ethical Boundaries:** Influence isn't inherently bad, but it must be transparent and respectful.

✅ **Practice Critical Thinking:** Stay curious and challenge claims, especially from charismatic figures.

✅ **Build Strong Support Systems:** Groups that discourage independent thought often want control.

✅ **Monitor Your Biases:** We're all vulnerable to tribalism, celebrity worship, and social validation. Be aware.

☀ The Quick & Dirty

1 Manipulation is rarely loud. It's subtle, emotional, and often feels like your idea.

2 Politicians and marketers use your emotions to control your attention, beliefs, and choices.

3 Cult-like control exists outside of cults—watch for isolation, blind loyalty, and savior figures.

4 Celebrities and influencers don't just sell products—they sell identities.

5 Psychological warfare happens in boardrooms, locker rooms, and social feeds. Stay sharp.

6 If something feels "too obvious," "too urgent," or "too emotional"—that's your cue to slow down.

7 Influence is given, not stolen. Take back the wheel by questioning your reactions.

8 Awareness is defense. Once you see the strings, you stop dancing to someone else's tune.

CHAPTER 12
DEFENSIVE AND EMPOWERMENT STRATEGIES

> " *"When you acquire enough inner peace and feel really positive about yourself, it's almost impossible for you to be controlled and manipulated by anybody else."*
>
> *~ Wayne Dyer*

Hey, so what's the chapter summary for 🔐 "Defensive and Empowerment Strategies"? LMK

Hey, you made it! FR This is the final chapter 📖 and it ties together everything you've learned about dark psychology and flips the focus toward protection, empowerment, and ethical self-mastery. The goal? Not just to defend against manipulation—but to thrive.

🧠 KNOW THYSELF: PSYCHOLOGICAL SELF-DISCOVERY

- **Self-awareness is your first defense.** Understand your unique psychological profile using tools like the Big Five, MBTI, and journaling.
- **Track emotional triggers and patterns** via reflection and journaling prompts. Ask yourself what situations spark anxiety, confidence, or frustration.
- **Watch out for cognitive biases** like confirmation bias or the halo effect, which can cloud decision-making and make you easier to manipulate.
- **Identify your blind spots** by seeking honest feedback from trusted friends and colleagues.

👉 *Takeaway: Self-awareness helps you recognize emotional manipulation and reduces your vulnerability to external influence.*

💪 EMOTIONAL RESILIENCE: BECOMING MENTALLY UNSHAKEABLE

- **Resilience = Your Emotional Armor.** It helps you recover from stress, think clearly under pressure, and handle manipulative tactics with poise.
- **Journaling, Meditation, Mindfulness, and CBT Techniques** like reframing and visualization all build resilience.
- **Practice Breathing Techniques** (e.g., box breathing) and daily affirmations to reinforce emotional strength.
- **Prioritize Self-Care:** Exercise, sleep, and nutrition are foundational to emotional well-being.

👉 *Takeaway: A calm mind and balanced body are much harder to manipulate.*

💡 COUNTERING PERSUASION WITH CONFIDENCE

- **Confidence is the antidote to coercion.** If you trust yourself, it's hard for others to sway your decisions.
- **Use visualization techniques** help you rehearse confident behavior.
- **Celebrate small wins** to build momentum and inner belief.
- **Sharpen critical thinking skills** by questioning logic, spotting bias, and evaluating motives.

👉 *Takeaway: A confident, critically-thinking person can see through manipulative tactics and stand firm in their decisions.*

🚧 SETTING BOUNDARIES: ASSERTIVENESS IS YOUR SECRET WEAPON

- **Boundaries protect your time, energy, and values.** Think of them as invisible fences keeping toxic influences out.
- **Assertiveness ≠ Aggression.** It's expressing your needs calmly and clearly, while respecting others.
- **Use "I" statements** (e.g., "I feel overwhelmed when ...") to avoid sounding accusatory.
- **Consistency matters.** If you set a boundary, honor it—no exceptions.

👉 *Takeaway: Clear boundaries are a powerful defense mechanism that signal to others you can't be easily controlled.*

🛡 ADVANCED ASSERTIVENESS: VERBAL SELF-DEFENSE

- **Assertiveness is a learned skill.** Practice makes it easier and more natural.
- **Learn to say "no" without guilt** or over-explaining. Your time and energy are finite.
- **Adapt your boundaries over time** based on feedback and changing needs.

👉 *Takeaway: Verbal assertiveness creates space for self-respect while shutting down manipulation early.*

🌱 ETHICAL PERSUASION: LIGHT-SIDE DARK PSYCHOLOGY

- **Dark tactics can be used ethically** in leadership, coaching, and communication when rooted in honesty and integrity.
- **Ethical influence is about mutual benefit**, not control or deceit.
- **Use principles like:**
  - Reciprocity (offer value first)
  - Authority (share expertise authentically)
  - Scarcity (truthfully highlight urgency)
  - Framing (positive, forward-thinking language)
  - Social Proof (honest testimonials)
  - Commitment (ask for small steps first)

👉 *Takeaway: Ethical persuasion is powerful and persuasive—without compromising your values.*

🖐 ENHANCING TEAM DYNAMICS

- **Mirroring builds rapport** and helps teams align quickly.
- **Emotional validation** shows respect and keeps morale high.
- **Anchoring and refocusing** help resolve conflict smoothly.
- **Subliminal motivation** through language, symbols, and reinforcement creates culture and cohesion.

👉 *Takeaway: Leaders who ethically use influence techniques create safe, effective, and high-performing teams.*

📈 CAREER ADVANCEMENT

- **Perception management** and branding help you control how others see you.
- **Strategic self-disclosure** builds trust while maintaining professionalism.
- **Leverage associations** with thought leaders to elevate your status.
- **Frame your success stories** with clear data and positive outcomes.

👉 *Takeaway: Using psychological tactics ethically in your career can create opportunities without manipulation.*

🏅 SPORTS PSYCHOLOGY: WINNING THE MENTAL GAME

- **Mental toughness training** preps athletes to handle pressure and adversity.
- **Focus anchoring, visualization, and breathing** reinforce peak performance.
- **Positive reinforcement** builds team morale and long-term excellence.

👉 *Takeaway: Mindset is everything—when athletes master the inner game, performance naturally improves.*

🎮 MIND CONTROL FOR SELF-IMPROVEMENT

- **Reframe limiting beliefs** into empowering truths.
- **Use self-anchoring** to trigger confidence, calm, or focus.
- **Affirmations and visualization** help embed positive beliefs.
- **Emotional control** reduces reactivity and sharpens clarity.

👉 *Takeaway: Mind control isn't sinister when applied to your own growth—it's a self-mastery tool.*

🌀 HARNESSING NLP & HYPNOSIS

- **Self-hypnosis and NLP** help uncover subconscious patterns, shift behavior, and promote healing.
- **Guided sessions reduce stress, shift mindset, and reinforce desired behaviors.**

- **Applications:** breaking bad habits, boosting confidence, managing stress.

👉 *Takeaway: Hypnosis and NLP can support personal transformation when used mindfully and ethically.*

☀ *The Quick & Dirty*

1. Self-awareness and emotional intelligence are your strongest defenses.

2. Assertiveness, boundaries, and confidence are daily tools for mental empowerment.

3. Ethical use of dark psychology techniques amplifies your ability to lead, inspire, and grow.

4. You don't have to be manipulative to be powerful—you just need awareness, discernment, and courage.

CHAPTER 13

CONCLUSION: FROM PAWN TO GRANDMASTER

> " *They built their power on your ignorance and played chess with your emotions. Now that you have the playbook and are no longer a pawn, guess who's the Grandmaster?*"
>
> ~ *Wynne Wick*

Hey, tell me more about the conclusion: "From Pawn to Grandmaster" ☀️ NGL I'm curious!

Hey congrats! You did it! 🙌 You've completed an extraordinary journey through the hidden world of dark psychology. This final chapter isn't just a reflection—it's a rallying cry. You are no longer a passive target for manipulation. You're equipped, empowered, and enlightened. ICYMI - here's the scoop!

⭐ PURPOSE REVISITED: WHY THIS BOOK EVEN EXISTS

- This book is designed to **lift the veil** on manipulation and psychological control.
- The goal isn't fear—it is **freedom**. Not paranoia, but **power** through awareness.
- The methods discussed aren't just theoretical—they are **real, practical, and visible** in everyday interactions.
- Manipulation only works when you don't see it. Now you do. 💥

👉 *Takeaway: Knowledge kills deception. You are no longer an easy mark.*

🔍 WHAT YOU'VE LEARNED (AKA YOUR PSYCHOLOGICAL ARSENAL)

Throughout the chapters, you've mastered essential defensive and offensive tools. Here's a quick recap of what you now know:

🧠 **Human Behavior & Psychological Profiling**

- Understand the **Dark Triad** (narcissism, Machiavellianism, psychopathy) and personality traits like those in the **Big Five** or **HEXACO**.
- Recognize manipulation based on **behavioral patterns** and **motivational cues**.

🕴 **Body Language & Nonverbal Cues**

- Read people through **micro-expressions,** posture shifts, eye contact, and facial cues.
- See how others communicate without words—and how you can project strength without speaking.

🕵️ **Detecting Deception**

- Identify lies through **inconsistencies**, increased **cognitive load**, and **verbal leakage.**
- Use techniques from interrogation science like **Reid and PEACE models.**

💔 **Emotional Manipulation**

- Recognize tools like **gaslighting, love bombing, emotional blackmail,** and **guilt-tripping.**
- Use your emotional intelligence as both a radar and a shield.

😎 **Covert Influence & Persuasion Tactics**

- Spot manipulation through **scarcity, social proof, commitment,** and **framing.**
- Stay alert to psychological warfare in everyday media and relationships.

🌀 **Mind Control, NLP, and Hypnosis**

- Understand **anchoring, priming, suggestion,** and **pattern interruption.**
- Learn how **language patterns** and hypnotic techniques bypass your conscious filters.

📱 **Digital and Social Media Manipulation**

- Detect **algorithmic bias, targeted ads,** and **influencer persuasion.**
- Guard your attention like a sacred currency.

🌐 Real-World Applications

- Identify manipulation in **politics, marketing, cults, celebrity culture,** and **competitive spaces.**
- Learn how these systems subtly shape our beliefs and behaviors.

👉 *Takeaway: You now have **eyes to see the invisible strings** being pulled in every domain of life.*

💡 ETHICAL REMINDERS: USE THESE POWERS FOR GOOD

- Yes, you could manipulate people. But should you?
- Always ground your actions in **integrity, authenticity,** and **mutual benefit.**
- Ethical persuasion is about **guidance,** not **domination.**
- Influence can be healing when used responsibly.

👉 *Takeaway: Influence without ethics is exploitation. With ethics, it becomes transformation.*

🔄 INTEGRATION: APPLYING YOUR KNOWLEDGE DAILY

You don't need a stage or a classroom to apply what you've learned. The world is your lab. 🌐

In your daily life:

- Use **micro-expression reading** in conversations to catch hidden feelings.
- Protect yourself from **emotional manipulation** in personal relationships.
- Set **strong boundaries** at work to resist guilt-based or passive-aggressive tactics.
- **Stay critical and calm** during sales pitches, political debates, or social media campaigns.
- **Reflect often:** "Is this persuasion ... or manipulation?"

👉 *Takeaway: Every interaction is a chance to apply your skills, sharpen your awareness, and choose clarity over confusion.*

📚 LIFELONG LEARNING: THIS IS JUST THE BEGINNING

- Dark psychology is ever-evolving—so should your awareness.
- Revisit tools, activities, and reflection prompts.
- Explore, stay curious, and **keep questioning everything**.
- Join communities, forums, or masterminds to continue exploring with others.

- Stay informed about emerging tactics (e.g., AI-driven persuasion, deepfake deception, etc.).

👉 *Takeaway: Mental strength is like muscle—it grows with consistent reps. Keep training.* 💪

👄 CONNECT AND EMPOWER OTHERS

- Share your knowledge responsibly with friends, family, and clients.
- Be the one who breaks toxic cycles in relationships and teams.
- Model critical thinking, emotional boundaries, and confident communication.
- Build **a tribe of psychologically aware people** who uplift rather than exploit.

👉 *Takeaway: Empowered people empower people. You can now be a beacon for others still lost in the fog.*

🎯 Bullseye Recap

- The greatest manipulators rely on your **insecurity, confusion, and self-doubt**.
- Now you have clarity, self-knowledge, and choice.
- You've gone from pawn to player ... to **Grandmaster**.

✅ **Final Takeaways:**

- **You are not powerless.**
- **You are not naïve.**
- **You are not easily fooled.**

👉 *You are ready. Stay sharp, stay ethical, and stay true to yourself.*

🎓 YOUR GRADUATION QUOTE:

❝❝ *"Your focus determines your reality."*

Qui-Gon Jinn

💪 Now, go forth and see clearly. Manipulation is only powerful in the shadows. You've just turned on the spotlight.

CHAPTER 14
BONUS SECTION

🎁 **B**onus Section: ~~25~~ ~~35~~ Secret NLP Tips for Mastering Influence and Communication

1. LEVERAGE EMOTIONAL TRIGGERS FOR PERSUASION

🔐 **Key Points:**

- Tune into the emotional drivers behind decisions (e.g., pride, fear, joy).
- Use active listening and probing questions to uncover someone's emotional landscape.
- Tailor your message to appeal directly to the emotions you've identified (e.g., status, security, recognition).
- Handle emotional triggers with sensitivity to preserve trust and authenticity.

⭐ *Takeaway: When you align your message with someone's emotional core, you unlock powerful influence—just make sure it's done ethically and with empathy.*

2. UTILIZE THE "HANDSHAKE INTERRUPT" TECHNIQUE

🔓 **Key Points:**

- Disrupt a routine action (like a handshake) to snap someone into heightened awareness.
- Introduce a slight change—such as lingering or altering grip —to break the pattern.
- Follow the interruption with a confident suggestion or embedded command.
- Use this technique subtly and sparingly to avoid coming off as manipulative.

⭐ *Takeaway: A well-timed disruption of a physical habit can make someone more suggestible—if used wisely, it opens a brief window for deep influence.*

3. MASTER "CONVERSATIONAL LEADING" THROUGH STORYTELLING

🔓 **Key Points:**

- Use stories to bypass resistance and plant ideas indirectly.
- Include a relatable character, a struggle, and a resolution aligned with your goal.
- Emotional, sensory storytelling helps people identify with the message.
- Practice delivering stories naturally to build rapport and guide perception.

⭐ *Takeaway: Stories sneak past defenses and speak directly to the heart—lead people by letting them walk through a story, not a lecture.*

4. USE EMBEDDED COMMANDS

🔓 **Key Points:**

- Slip subtle commands inside normal conversation (e.g., "You might start feeling more relaxed …").
- Use tone, pauses, or gestures to highlight the command without being obvious.
- Plan your desired outcome and weave it naturally into dialogue.
- Works best in relaxed, trust-filled environments.

⭐ *Takeaway: When embedded within casual speech, subtle suggestions can steer thoughts without setting off alarms.*

5. LEVERAGE THE POWER OF "YES SETS"

🔓 **Key Points:**

- Start with easy questions or statements that prompt agreement.
- Build momentum with successive "yes" responses to lower resistance.
- Transition to your main idea after establishing a cooperative rhythm.
- Keep it natural—don't sound scripted or pushy.

⭐ *Takeaway: Agreement is contagious—stack enough small "yeses" and bigger agreements often follow.*

6. UTILIZE THE "AS IF" FRAME

🔓 **Key Points:**

- Encourage someone to act "as if" they already had the confidence, success, or clarity they seek.
- Ask questions like, "What would you do if this were already solved?"
- Shifts mindset from doubt to action by engaging imagination.
- Useful in coaching, problem-solving, and confidence-building.

⭐ *Takeaway: When people act "as if" they already have what they want, they start creating it.*

7. CREATE FUTURE PACING STATEMENTS

🔓 **Key Points:**

- Paint a vivid mental picture of success tied to a specific outcome.
- Use sensory details to make the experience feel real (sights, sounds, emotions).
- Future pacing boosts motivation by bridging now with what's possible.
- Especially powerful in goal-setting and inspiration.

⭐ *Takeaway: People move toward the future they can clearly imagine—help them see it, feel it, and believe it.*

8. USE HYPNOTIC LANGUAGE PATTERNS

🔓 **Key Points:**

- Speak with rhythm and calm tone to lower resistance.
- Use phrasing like "As you begin to notice ..." or "You might start feeling ..." to gently lead thoughts.
- Pair with eye contact and pauses to deepen impact.
- Works best when woven into normal conversation.

⭐ *Takeaway: Hypnotic phrasing can plant seeds of belief and behavior change—without a single argument.*

9. FRAME CONVERSATIONS POSITIVELY

🔒 **Key Points:**

- Reframe negative language into growth-oriented alternatives.
- Emphasize what can be gained rather than what's lost.
- Show understanding, then pivot toward opportunity or strength.
- Reframing reduces defensiveness and invites problem-solving.

⭐ *Takeaway: Change the frame, change the feeling—people respond better to what sounds empowering and possible.*

10. APPLY THE LAW OF REQUISITE VARIETY

🔒 **Key Points:**

- The most adaptable person in any interaction holds the most influence.
- Match the other person's energy, tone, and language—then gradually guide it.
- Read the room and adjust in real-time.
- Flexibility builds trust and keeps conversations fluid.

⭐ *Takeaway: If you can shift your approach, you can shift the outcome—adaptability is real power.*

11. USE SPATIAL ANCHORS

🔓 **Key Points:**

- Assign specific physical spaces to emotions, decisions, or types of content.
- For example, stand in one spot when delivering praise and another when discussing problems.
- Consistency strengthens the emotional association.
- Works especially well in presentations, coaching, and negotiations.

⭐ *Takeaway: Where you stand can shape how people feel—anchor emotions to spaces to guide responses.*

12. ELICIT AND UTILIZE VALUES

🔓 **Key Points:**

- Ask open-ended questions to discover what someone truly values (e.g., freedom, security, growth).
- Align your message or offer with those values to reduce resistance.
- Reflect those values back in language that feels personalized.
- Builds deeper trust and resonance.

⭐ *Takeaway: When you speak to someone's values, you speak to their soul—values are the gateway to influence.*

13. CHUNK INFORMATION STRATEGICALLY

🔓 **Key Points:**

- Chunk up to simplify: group related ideas under a broader theme.
- Chunk down to clarify: break complex ideas into bite-sized steps.
- Prevents overwhelm and boosts clarity.
- Adapt your chunking based on the listener's knowledge level.

⭐ *Takeaway: Structure is power—chunking helps people absorb, remember, and act on what you say.*

14. USE METAPHORS AND STORIES

🔓 **Key Points:**

- Metaphors make abstract concepts tangible and memorable.
- Stories engage both logic and emotion, lowering resistance.
- Rich sensory details (sight, sound, feeling) deepen immersion.
- Audiences often adopt ideas presented through story without argument.

⭐ *Takeaway: Tell it well and they'll feel it—metaphors and stories speak in a language the brain loves.*

15. EMPLOY THE "DOUBLE BIND" TECHNIQUE

🔓 **Key Points:**

- Present two options that both lead to your desired outcome.

- Avoid offering a yes/no choice when you want movement.
- Keep both options positive and appealing to preserve trust.
- Use with care—too much can feel manipulative.

⭐ *Takeaway: Let them choose their path—just make sure every road leads where you want them to go.*

16. DEVELOP SENSORY ACUITY

🔐 **Key Points:**

- Train yourself to notice micro-expressions, tone shifts, and subtle body language.
- Watch for discrepancies between words and behavior.
- Use this awareness to adjust your tone, pacing, or message on the fly.
- Builds emotional intelligence and persuasion agility.

⭐ *Takeaway: The subtle signals say more than words—see what others miss, and you'll guide what others feel.*

17. APPLY PATTERN INTERRUPTS TO BREAK HABITS

🔐 **Key Points:**

- Disrupt predictable patterns with unexpected questions, humor, or pauses.
- Creates a mental reset that opens space for new thinking.
- Works in emotional ruts, negative spirals, or rigid thinking.
- Can be verbal, physical, or situational.

⭐ *Takeaway: To change the direction of thought, first break the pattern—surprise is the gateway to shift.*

18. IDENTIFY AND BREAK LIMITING BELIEFS

🔓 **Key Points:**

- Help others recognize and question the beliefs that are holding them back.
- Ask evidence-based or reframing questions ("What if the opposite were true?").
- Highlight past successes to challenge negative narratives.
- Replace old beliefs with empowering alternatives.

⭐ *Takeaway: Limiting beliefs are mental cages—once questioned, they lose their power.*

19. UTILIZE TEMPORAL LANGUAGE

🔓 **Key Points:**

- Shift focus between past (proof), present (action), and future (outcome) to reframe thinking.
- Use past successes to build confidence.
- Anchor present challenges to future rewards.
- Reduces anxiety and increases motivation.

⭐ *Takeaway: When people see their progress across time, they believe in the journey—and themselves.*

20. MASTER "META-MODEL" QUESTIONS

🔓 **Key Points:**

- Use specific, clarifying questions to challenge vague or limiting language.
- Break generalizations like "I always fail" with "Always? Can you think of one time you didn't?"

- Cuts through distortions and encourages accurate, resourceful thinking.
- Promotes accountability and problem-solving.

⭐ *Takeaway: Precision dismantles illusion—ask the right questions and fuzzy thoughts become clear action.*

21. UTILIZE NESTED LOOPS

🔐 **Key Points:**

- Begin a story or idea, then start another before finishing the first.
- Build suspense and curiosity by delaying resolution.
- Return to complete each loop in reverse order—this mirrors how people process layered thoughts.
- Enhances memory retention and emotional engagement.

⭐ *Takeaway: Tangle the thread, then tie it tight—nested loops keep people hooked and make your message stick.*

22. USE FRACTIONATION TO DEEPEN ENGAGEMENT

🔐 **Key Points:**

- Alternate between emotional intensity and lightness (e.g., deep then playful).
- Prevents emotional fatigue and creates dynamic contrast.
- Especially powerful in building rapport and romantic or high-stakes interactions.
- Keeps attention high and feelings vivid.

⭐ *Takeaway: We feel more deeply through contrast—mix depth with levity to create lasting emotional impact.*

23. MIRROR BREATHING PATTERNS

🔓 **Key Points:**

- Subtly match the rhythm of someone's breathing to build unconscious rapport.
- Once in sync, you can guide them into a calmer or more energized state.
- Particularly effective in stress, therapy, or negotiation settings.
- Requires observation and subtle execution.

⭐ *Takeaway: Breathe with them, lead with ease—mirror breath to mirror trust.*

24. LEVERAGE OPEN LOOPS IN CONVERSATION

🔓 **Key Points:**

- Introduce an unresolved idea or question early in a conversation.
- Delay closure to maintain attention and curiosity.
- Use in speeches, storytelling, or influence settings to drive engagement.
- The brain craves resolution—use that to your advantage.

⭐ *Takeaway: Leave them hanging (just a bit)—an open loop creates the itch that only you can scratch.*

25. USE THE "AGREEMENT FRAME"

🔓 **Key Points:**

- Acknowledge someone's viewpoint before guiding them to yours.

- Replace resistance with validation followed by redirection.
- Phrases like "I agree ... and" or "That makes sense ... what if" reduce defensiveness.
- Creates a collaborative tone, not a confrontational one.

⭐ *Takeaway: Agreement builds bridges—validate first, then walk them toward your side.*

26. PRACTICE THE "COLOMBO TECHNIQUE"

🔐 **Key Points:**

- Use curiosity and humility to lower defenses (e.g., "I could be wrong, but ...").
- Inspired by the disarming style of the TV detective, Lt. Colombo.
- Makes the other person more comfortable and open.
- Especially effective in negotiations, objections, and high-stakes conversations.

⭐ *Takeaway: Play curious, not clever—when you act like you're still figuring it out, people let their guard down.*

27. USE EMBEDDED SUGGESTIONS IN QUESTIONS

🔐 **Key Points:**

- Phrase questions to plant desirable beliefs or actions as assumptions.
- "How soon will you feel comfortable in your new role?" assumes they will.
- Shifts focus from *if* to *when* or *how*, reducing resistance.
- Presupposes success and influences mindset subtly.

⭐ *Takeaway: Shape the answer with your question—ask like it's already happening.*

28. CREATE "PERCEPTUAL POSITIONS"

🔓 **Key Points:**

- Explore a situation from three viewpoints: self, other person, neutral observer.
- Enhances empathy, perspective-taking, and emotional regulation.
- Helps resolve conflicts or make more objective decisions.
- Great in coaching and leadership contexts.

⭐ *Takeaway: Step outside yourself—perspective creates power and clarity.*

29. APPLY THE "SIX-STEP REFRAME"

🔓 **Key Points:**

- Identify a negative behavior and discover the positive intent behind it.
- Brainstorm alternative behaviors that fulfill the same need.
- Align subconscious intent with conscious goals.
- Useful for habit change, inner conflict, and coaching.

⭐ *Takeaway: Every unhelpful habit has a helpful root—find it, reframe it, replace it.*

30. ANCHOR CONFIDENCE WITH PHYSICAL CUES

🔓 **Key Points:**

- Pair a confident emotional state with a unique physical action (e.g., clenching a fist).
- Repeatedly reinforce this anchor during high-confidence moments.
- Later, trigger the anchor to instantly access that emotional state.
- Works especially well under pressure (e.g., public speaking, interviews).

⭐ *Takeaway: Confidence is portable—anchor it, and take it with you.*

31. USE SILENT PAUSES FOR IMPACT

🔓 **Key Points:**

- Pauses create anticipation and highlight key points.
- Silence invites the other person to fill the space—useful in negotiations.
- Conveys confidence and control when timed well.
- Helps listeners process and retain your message.

⭐ *Takeaway: Don't fear the pause—silence can speak louder than words.*

32. EMPLOY THE "BACKTRACK TECHNIQUE"

🔓 **Key Points:**

- Repeat or paraphrase what someone has just said to show you're listening.
- Builds trust, clarifies intent, and reduces miscommunication.
- Useful in conflict, coaching, and sales conversations.
- Creates opportunities to reinforce or redirect key points.

⭐ *Takeaway: Echo to connect—when people feel heard, they listen better too.*

33. USE THE "ELICITATION TECHNIQUE"

🔓 **Key Points:**

- Draw out hidden insights with gentle, open-ended questions.
- Avoid direct interrogation—use curiosity and interest.
- Great for uncovering motives, objections, or values.
- Builds rapport while gathering valuable intel.

⭐ *Takeaway: The right question reveals the truth—ask softly, learn deeply.*

34. PRIME POSITIVE OUTCOMES

🔓 **Key Points:**

- Set an optimistic tone at the beginning of an interaction.
- Frame challenges as opportunities and highlight past successes.
- Encourages solution-oriented thinking and receptiveness.
- Works well in leadership, coaching, and influence.

⭐ *Takeaway: Start positive, stay productive—priming optimism paves the path forward.*

35. VISUALIZE AND AMPLIFY SUCCESS

🔓 **Key Points:**

- Guide someone to vividly imagine their success with rich detail.
- Ask what they see, hear, feel at the moment of achievement.
- Builds belief, motivation, and emotional commitment.
- Useful in coaching, goal-setting, and performance prep.

⭐ *Takeaway: If they can picture it, they can pursue it—help them see success to **achieve** it.*

BIBLIOGRAPHY

- "Anchoring Effect." *Wikipedia*. Accessed January 28, 2025. https://en. wikipedia.org/wiki/Anchoring_effect.
- Ashton, Michael C., and Kibeom Lee. *The HEXACO Personality Inventory - Revised: A Measure of the Six Major Dimensions of Personality*. Accessed January 28, 2025. https://hexaco.org.
- "Best Practices for Security and Privacy Settings." *Stay Safe Online*. Accessed January 28, 2025. https://staysafeonline.org/resources/best-practices-for-security-and-privacy-settings/.
- Cialdini, Robert B. "Dr. Robert Cialdini's Seven Principles of Persuasion." *Influence at Work*. Accessed January 28, 2025. https://www.influenceatwork.com/7-principles-of-persuasion/.
- "Cialdini's 6 Principles of Influence - Definition and Examples." *Conceptually*. Accessed January 28, 2025. https://conceptually.org/concepts/6-principles-of-influence.
- "Cognitive Dissonance in Marketing | Definition, Theory." *Study.com*. Accessed January 28, 2025. https://study.com/academy/lesson/cognitive-dissonance-in-marketing-definition-examples-quiz.html.
- "Communication in Negotiation: Cialdini's Six Principles of Persuasion." *CMM LLP*. Accessed January 28, 2025. https://cmmllp.com/communication-in-negotiation-cialdinis-six-principles-of-persuasion/.
- "Cultural Differences in Body Language to Be Aware Of." *Virtual Speech*. Accessed January 28, 2025. https://virtualspeech.com/blog/cultural-differences-in-body-language.
- "Dealing with Workplace Manipulation." *Thriveworks*. Accessed January 28, 2025. https://thriveworks.com/blog/workplace-manipulation-identify-signs-communicate-effectively/.
- "Detecting Deception with Artificial Intelligence: Promises." *ScienceDirect*. Accessed January 28, 2025. https://www.sciencedirect.com/science/article/pii/S1364661324000810.
- "Dr. Robert Cialdini's Seven Principles of Persuasion." *Influence at Work*. Accessed January 28, 2025. https://www.influenceatwork.com/7-principles-of-persuasion/.
- Ekman, Paul. "Micro Expressions | Facial Expressions." *Paul Ekman Group*. Accessed January 28, 2025. https://www.paulekman.com/resources/micro-expressions/.

- "Gaslighting: Signs and Tips to Manage." *Healthline*. Accessed January 28, 2025. https://www.healthline.com/health/gaslighting.
- "Leadership Styles and Their Impact on Organizational Culture." *Medium*. Accessed January 28, 2025. https://medium.com/@contact_18616/leadership-styles-and-their-impact-on-organizational-culture-25d2d5ac9e74.
- "Manipulation in Relationships: Signs, Behaviors, & How to Spot." *Verywell Mind*. Accessed January 28, 2025. https://www.verywellmind.com/manipulation-in-marriage-2302245.
- "Manipulative Behavior: Signs, Definitions, and Tactics." *Verywell Health*. Accessed January 28, 2025. https://www.verywellhealth.com/manipulative-behavior-5214329.
- Pavlov, Skinner, and Bandura. "Learning Perspective on Development." *Nurse Key*. Accessed January 28, 2025. https://nursekey.com/pavlov-skinner-and-bandura-learning-perspective-on-development/.
- Pascual-Leone, Alvaro, et al. "Modulation of Muscle Responses Evoked by Transcranial Magnetic Stimulation During the Acquisition of New Fine Motor Skills." *Journal of Neurophysiology* 74, no. 3 (1995): 1037–45. https://doi.org/10.1152/jn.1995.74.3.1037.
- 7 Gaslighting Effects That You May Not Know - Gen Alpha World. https://hoomale.com/web-stories/7-gaslighting-effects-that-you-may-not-know/

www.ingramcontent.com/pod-product-compliance
Lightning Source LLC
Chambersburg PA
CBHW060209070426
42447CB00035B/2880